LETTER TRACING FOR KIDS

PEYTON

TRACE MY NAME WORKBOOK

Can't Find Your Name?

Have our elves create a personalized book with the name of your choice today!

VISIT US AT:

PersonalizeThisBook.com

Cover and page design by Cool Journals Studios - Copyright 2017

ABOUT ME

MY NAME IS:

Peyton

I LIVE IN:

For parents

For kids

I AM ☐ **YEARS OLD.**

DRAW YOU AND YOUR FAMILY

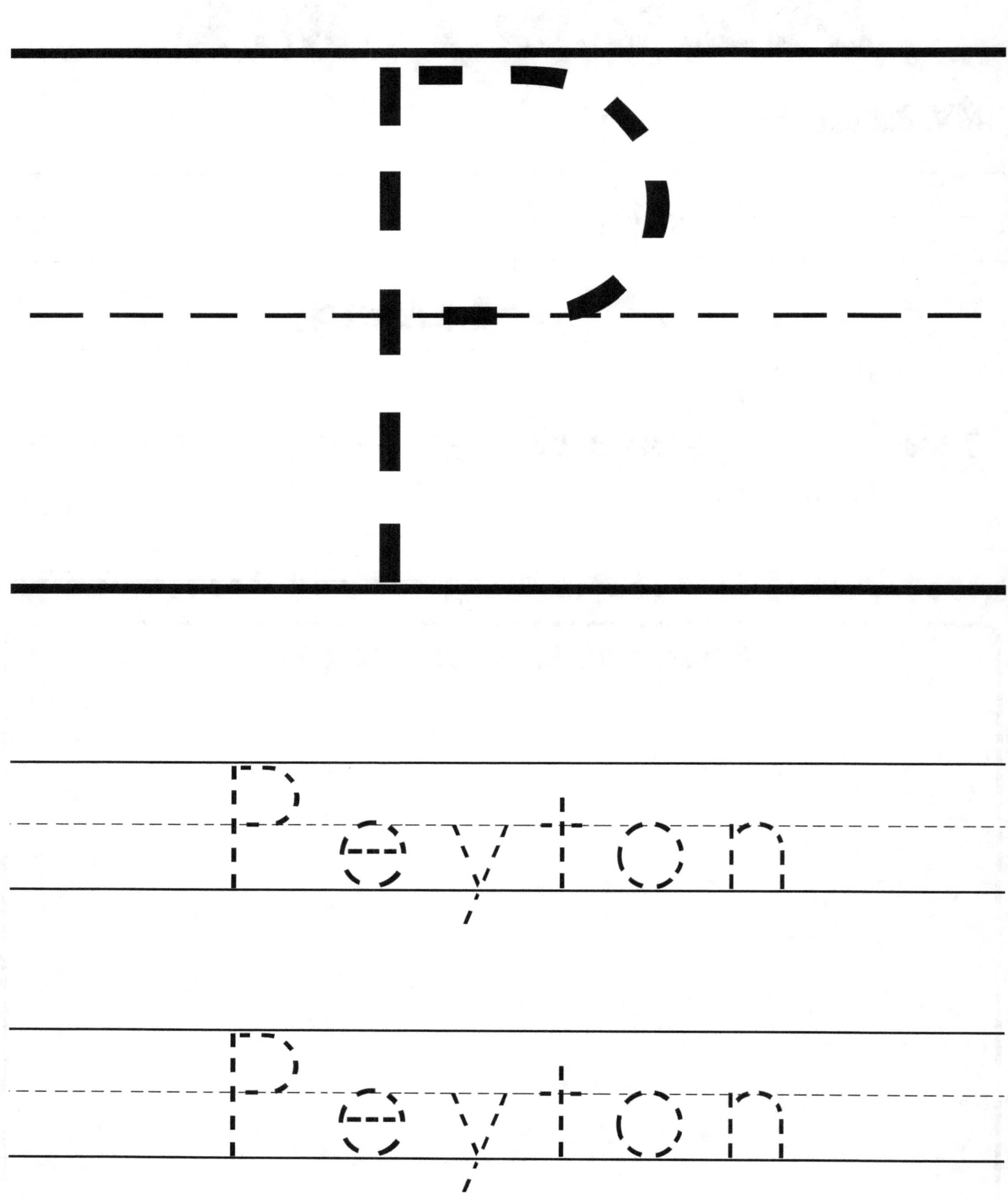

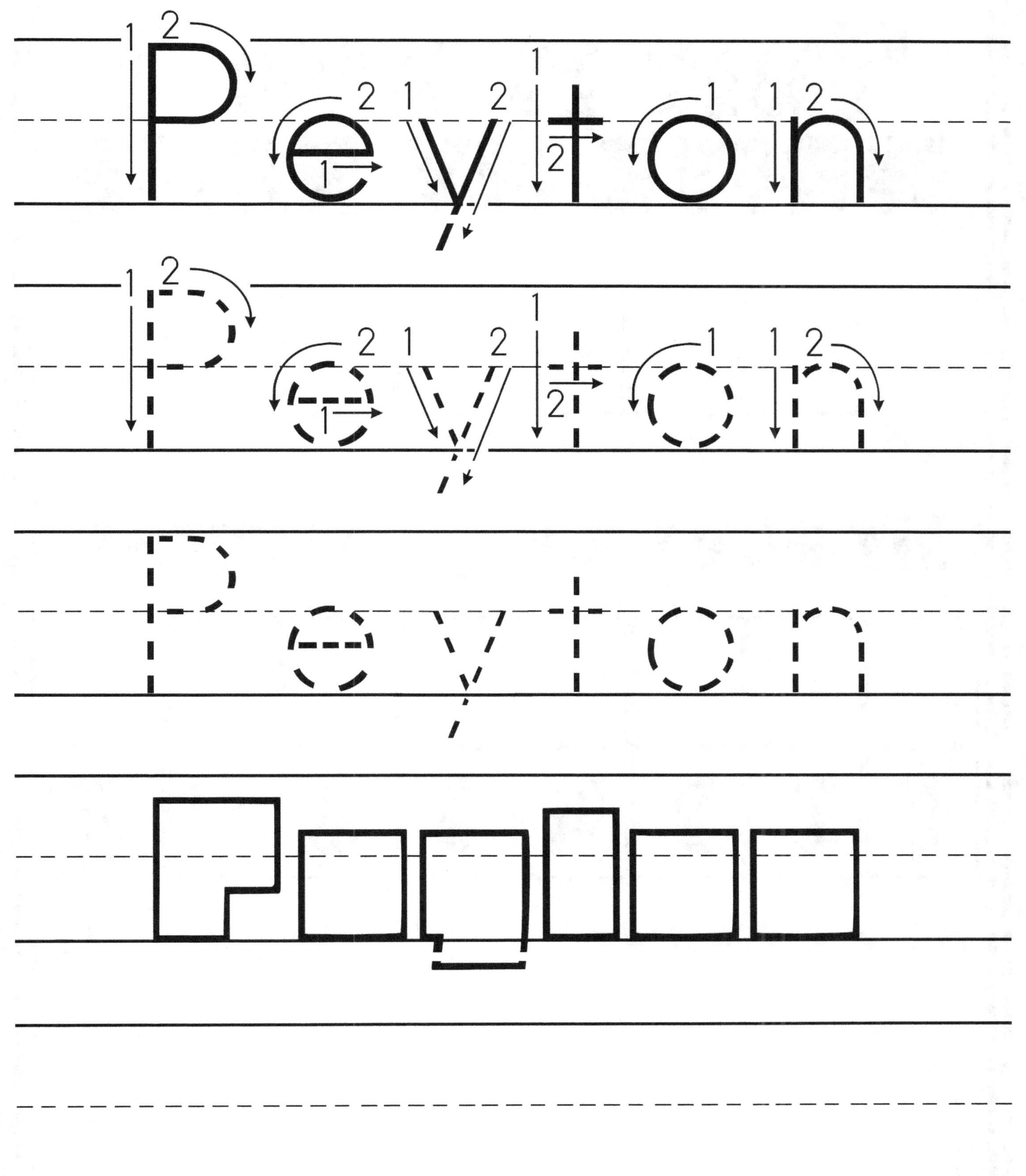

Peyton
Peyton
Peyton
Peyton

THIS IS HOW I WRITE MY NAME

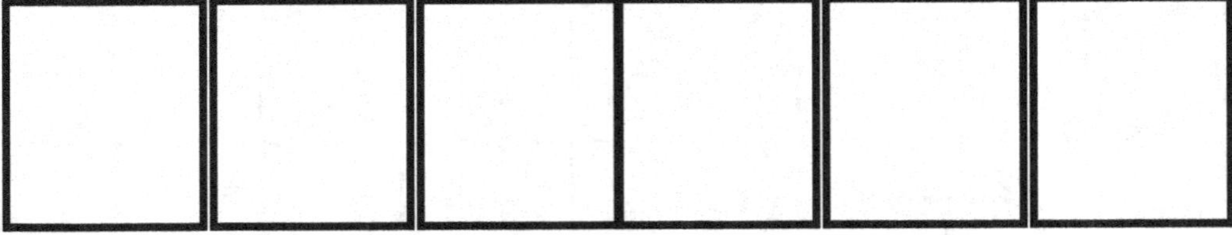

MY NAME HAS ___ LETTERS

1	2	3	4	5	6	7	8

Peyton
eyton
yton
ton
on
n

COLOR THE EGGS WITH LETTERS OF OUR NAME WRITE YOUR NAME

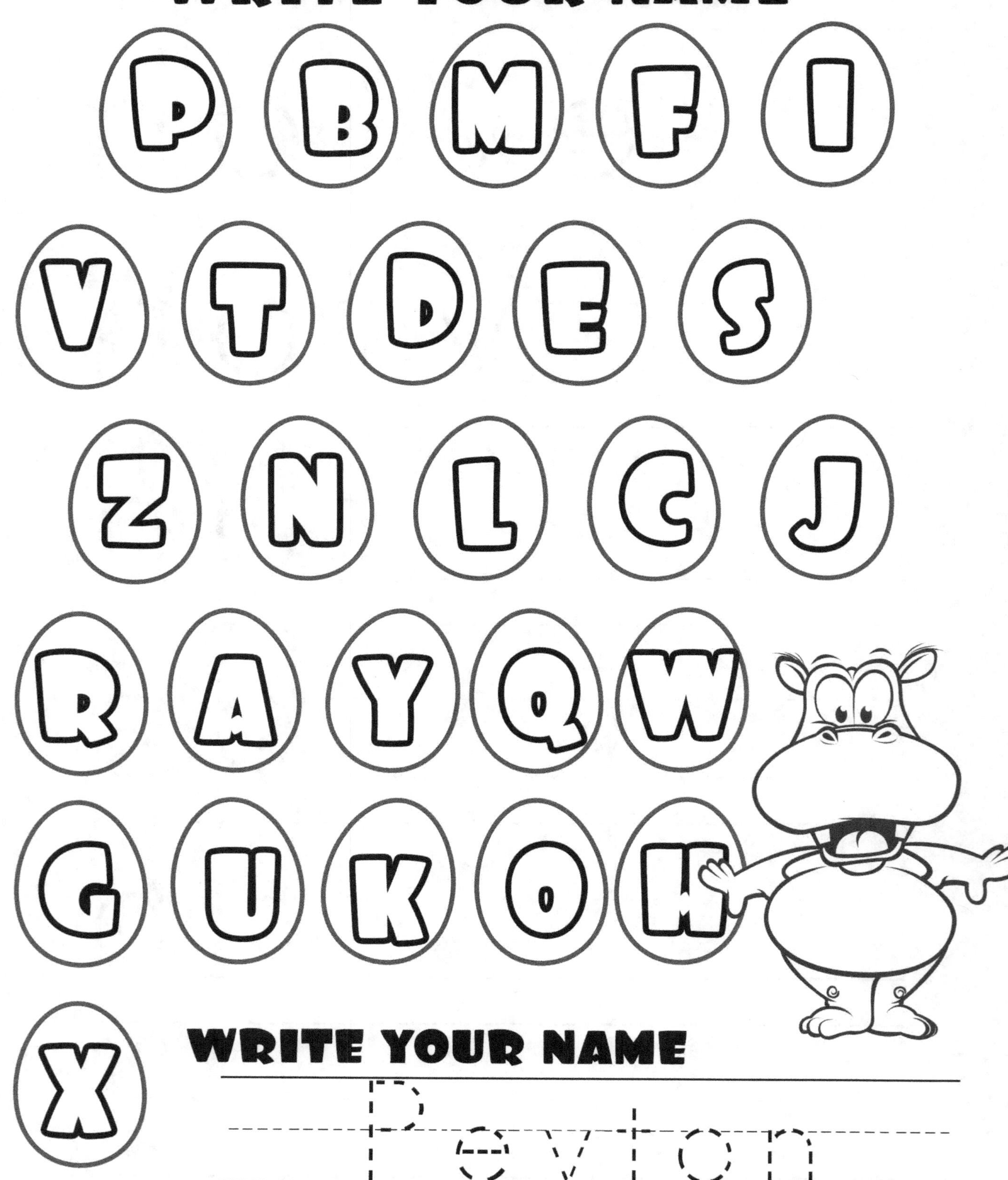

WRITE YOU NAME WITH,

PEN

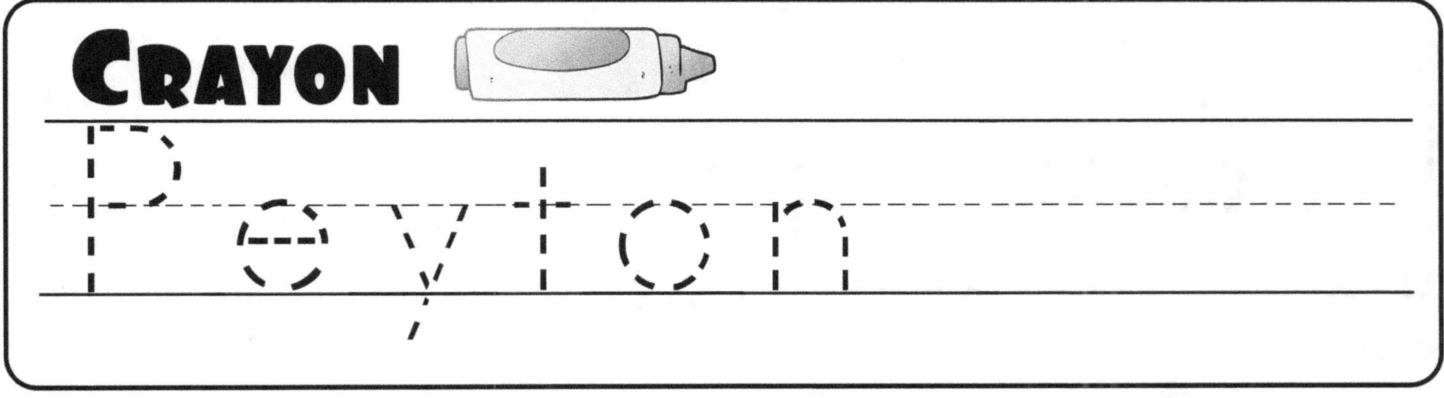

CRAYON

WRITE YOUR NAME IN BLUE

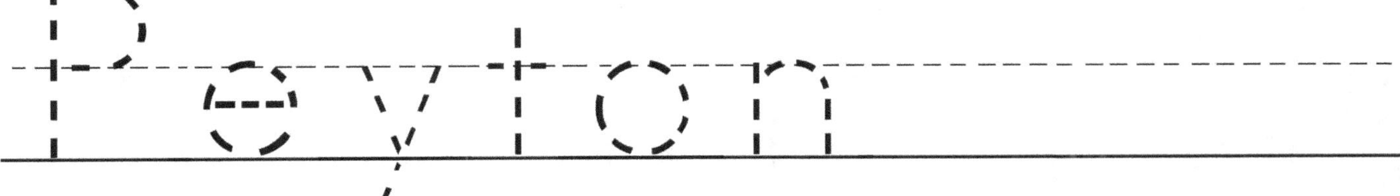

WRITE YOUR NAME IN YELLOW

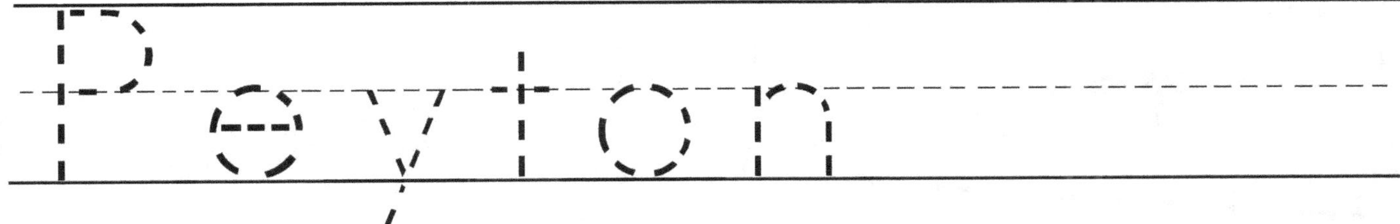

DRAW YOUR FAVORITE THINGS

COLOR

FOOD

TOY

ANIMAL

MY NAME

<table>
<tr><td>MY NAME
STARTS WITH

__________</td><td>MY NAME
ENDS WITH

__________</td></tr>
</table>

FILL THE LETTERS OF YOUR NAME WHITH DIFFERENT COLORS

P B W F V I T

D E S Z N L C

J R A Y Q K

G U X O H M

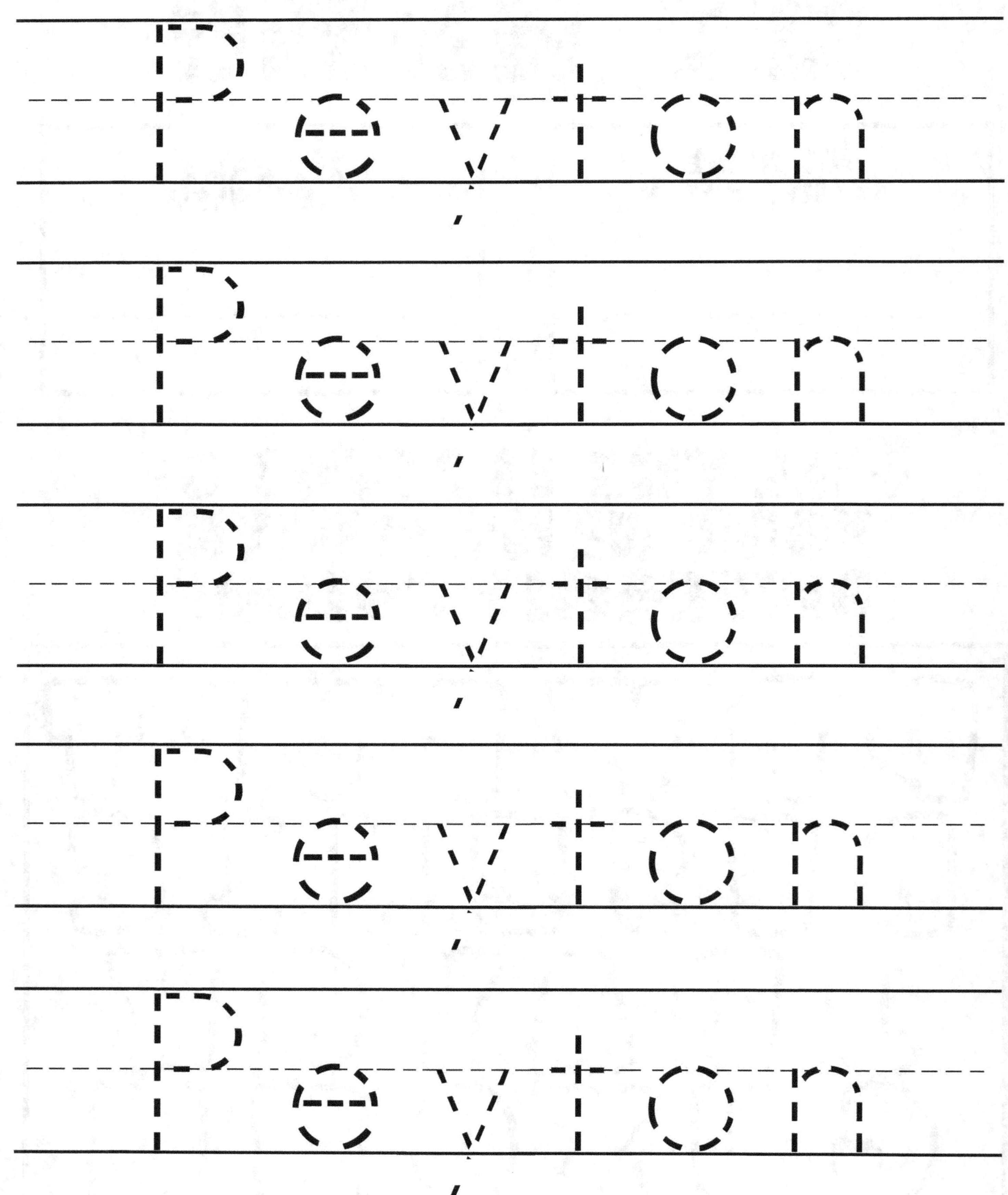

Peyton
Peyton
Peyton
Peyton
Peyton

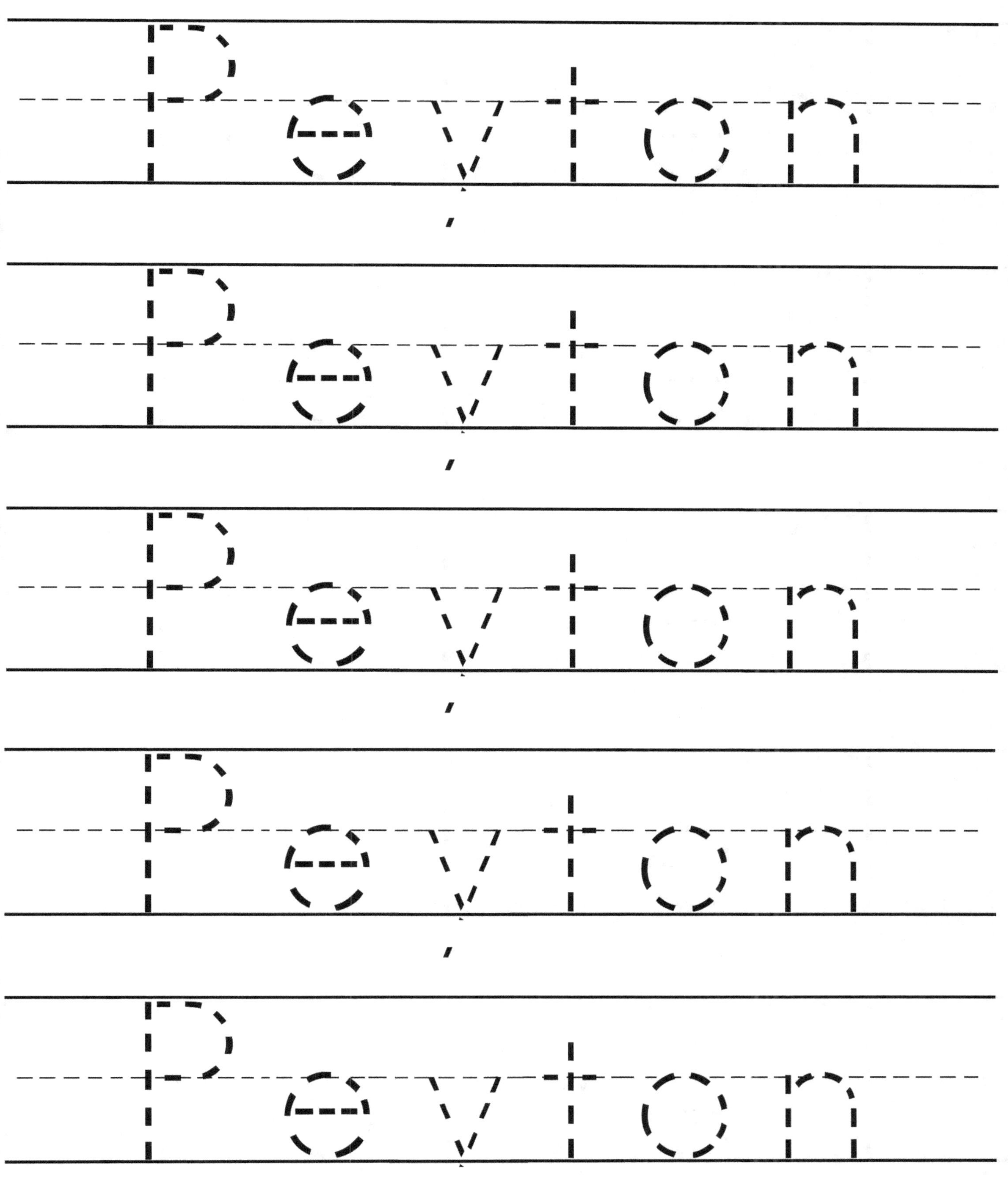

Peyton
Peyton
Peyton
Peyton
Peyton

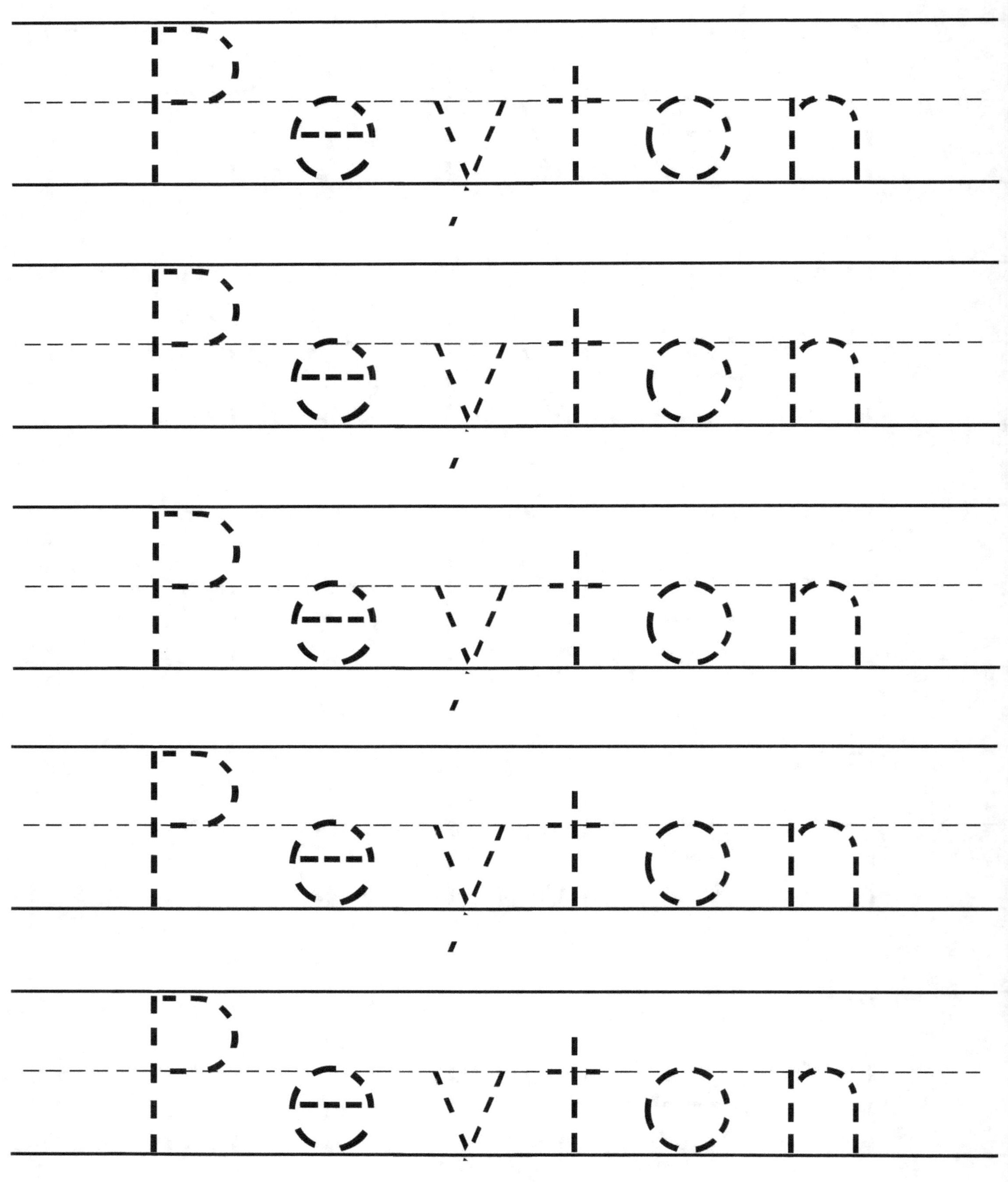

Peyton
Peyton
Peyton
Peyton
Peyton

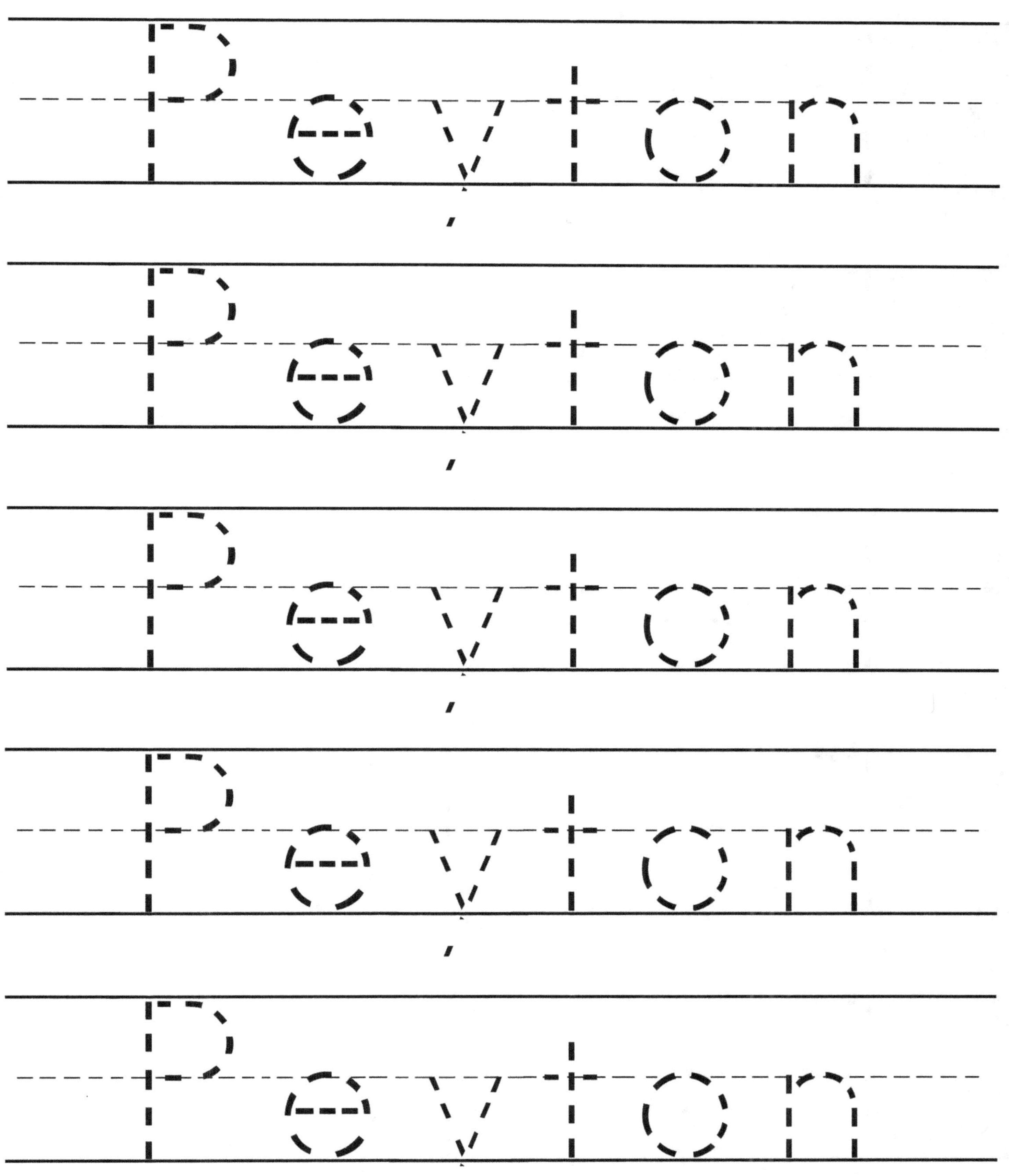

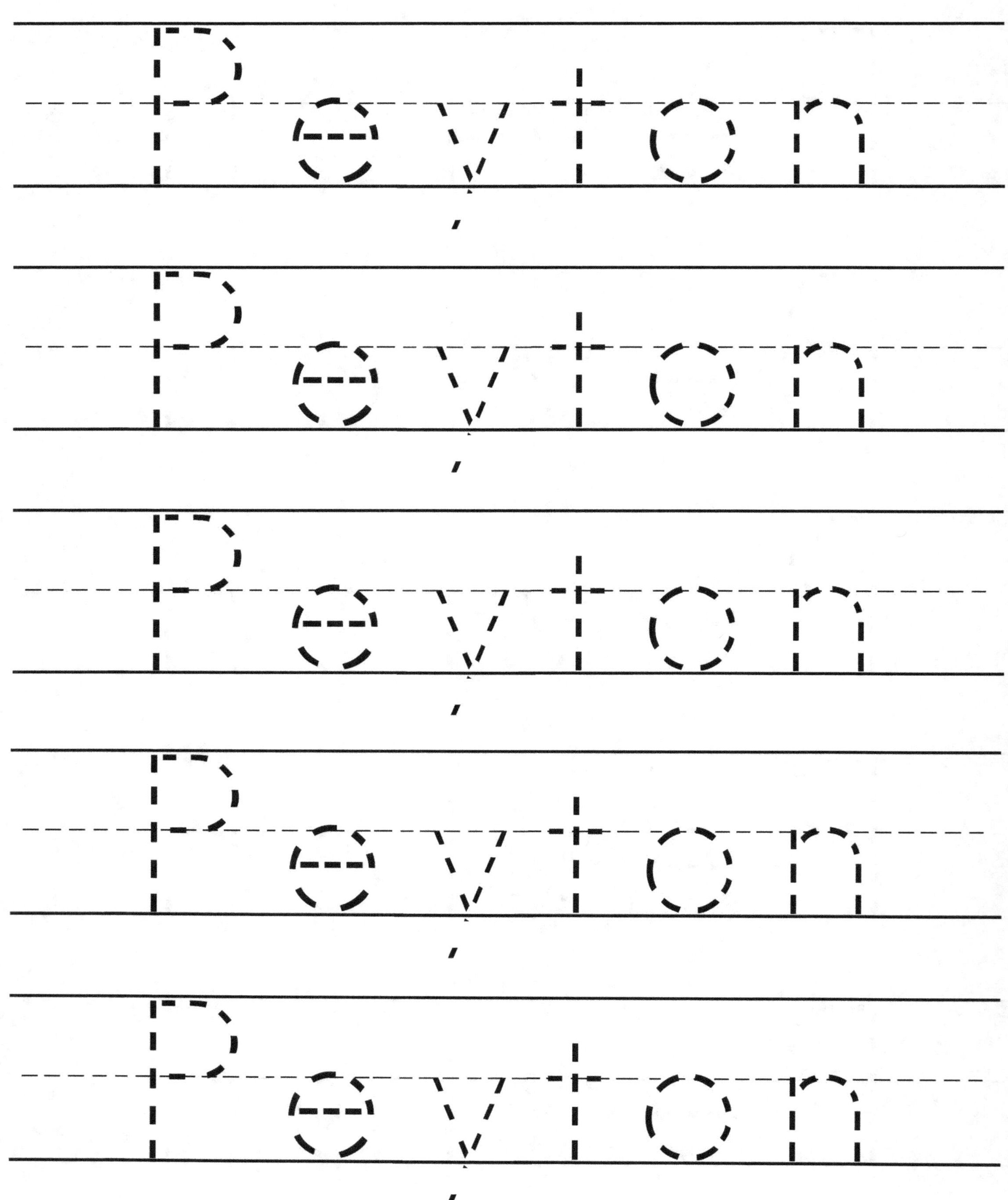

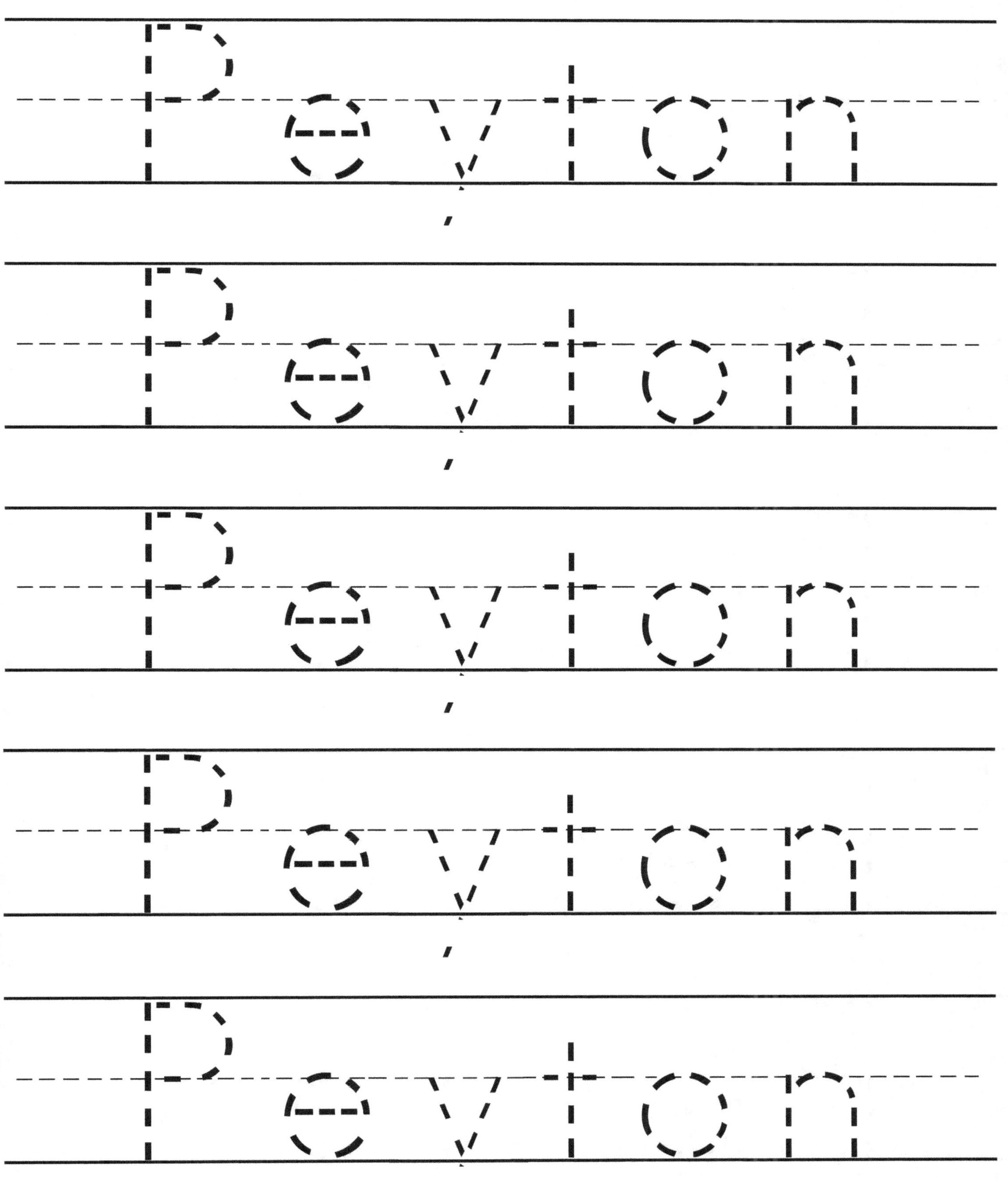

Peyton
Peyton
Peyton
Peyton
Peyton

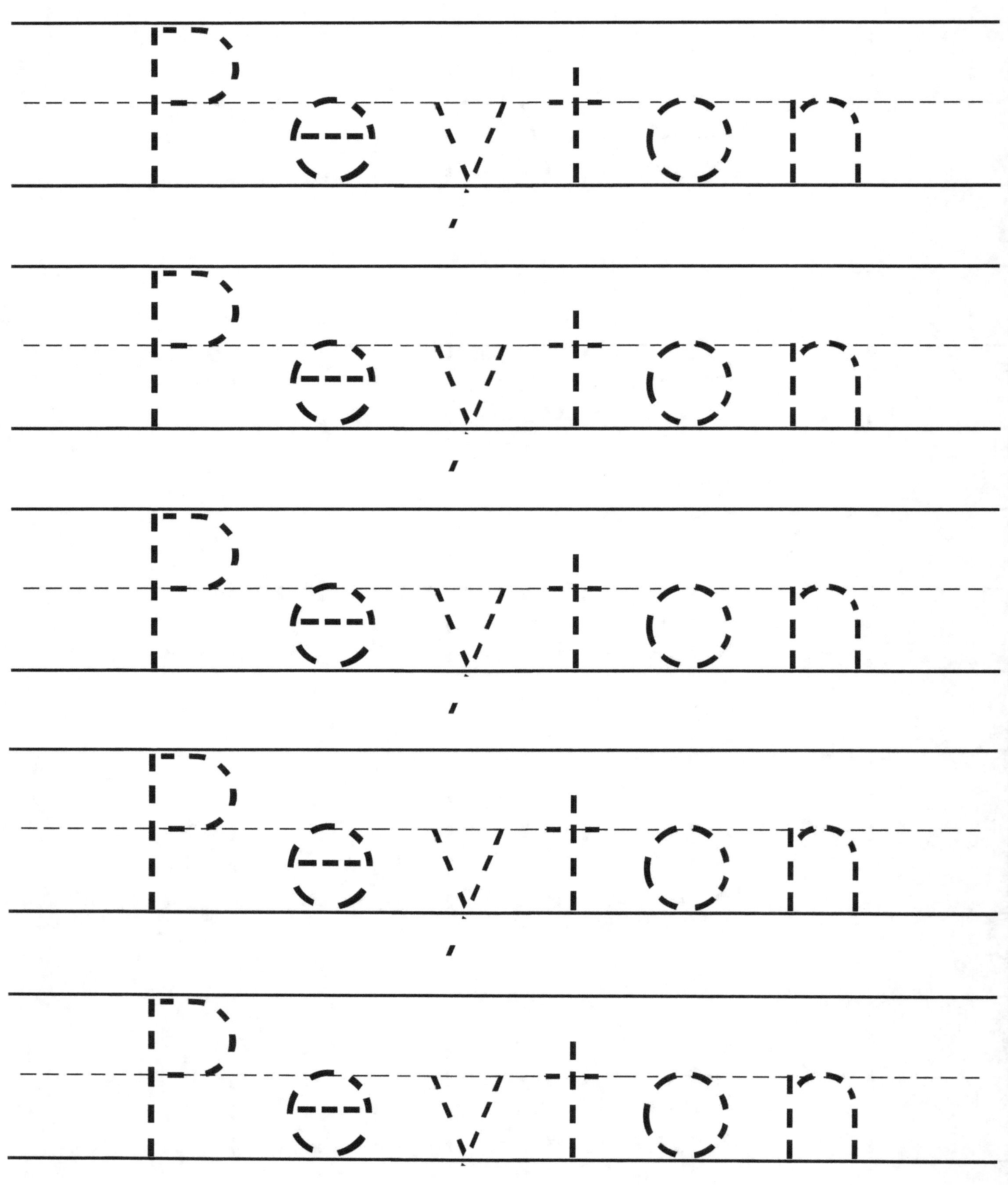

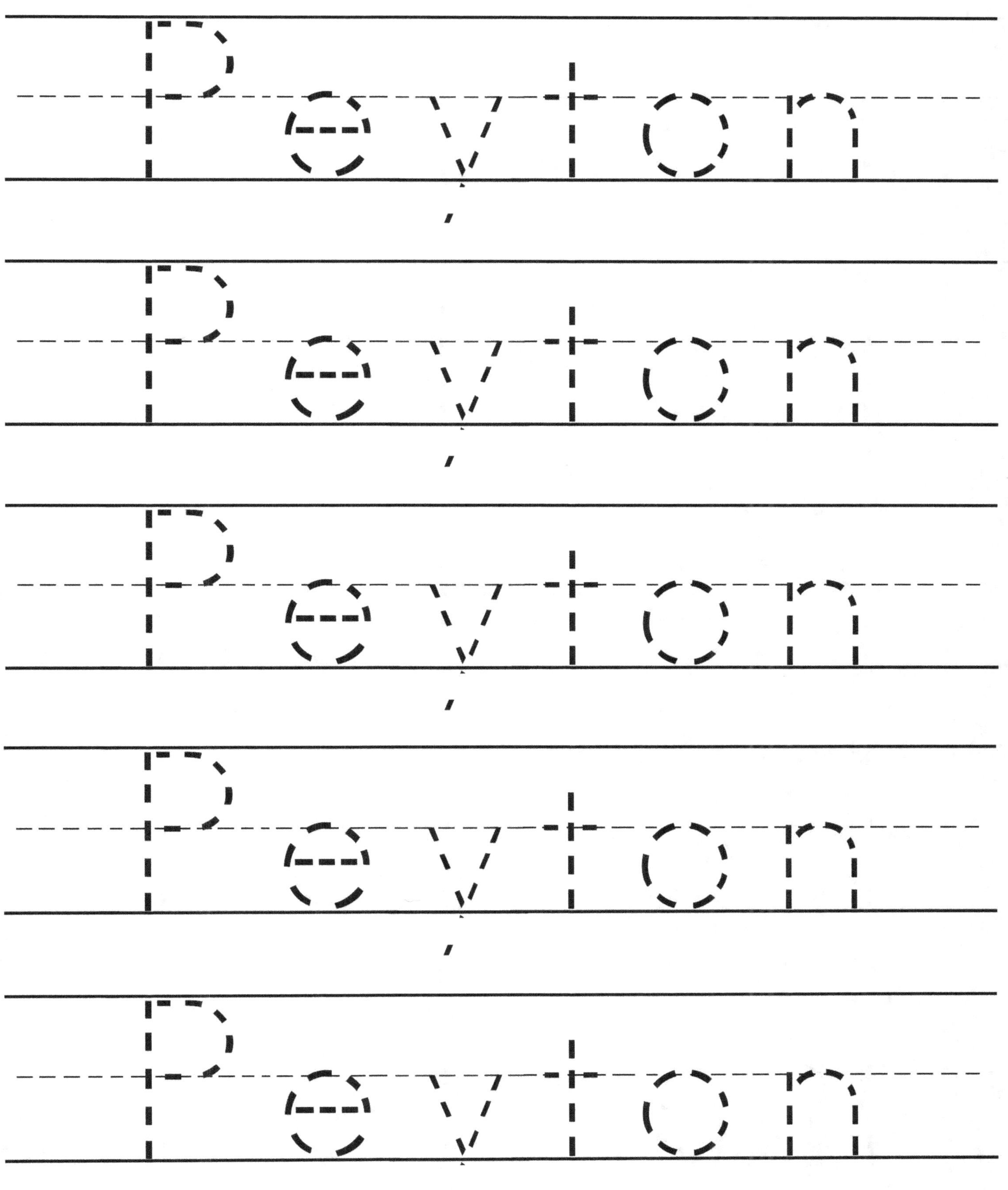
Peyton
Peyton
Peyton
Peyton
Peyton

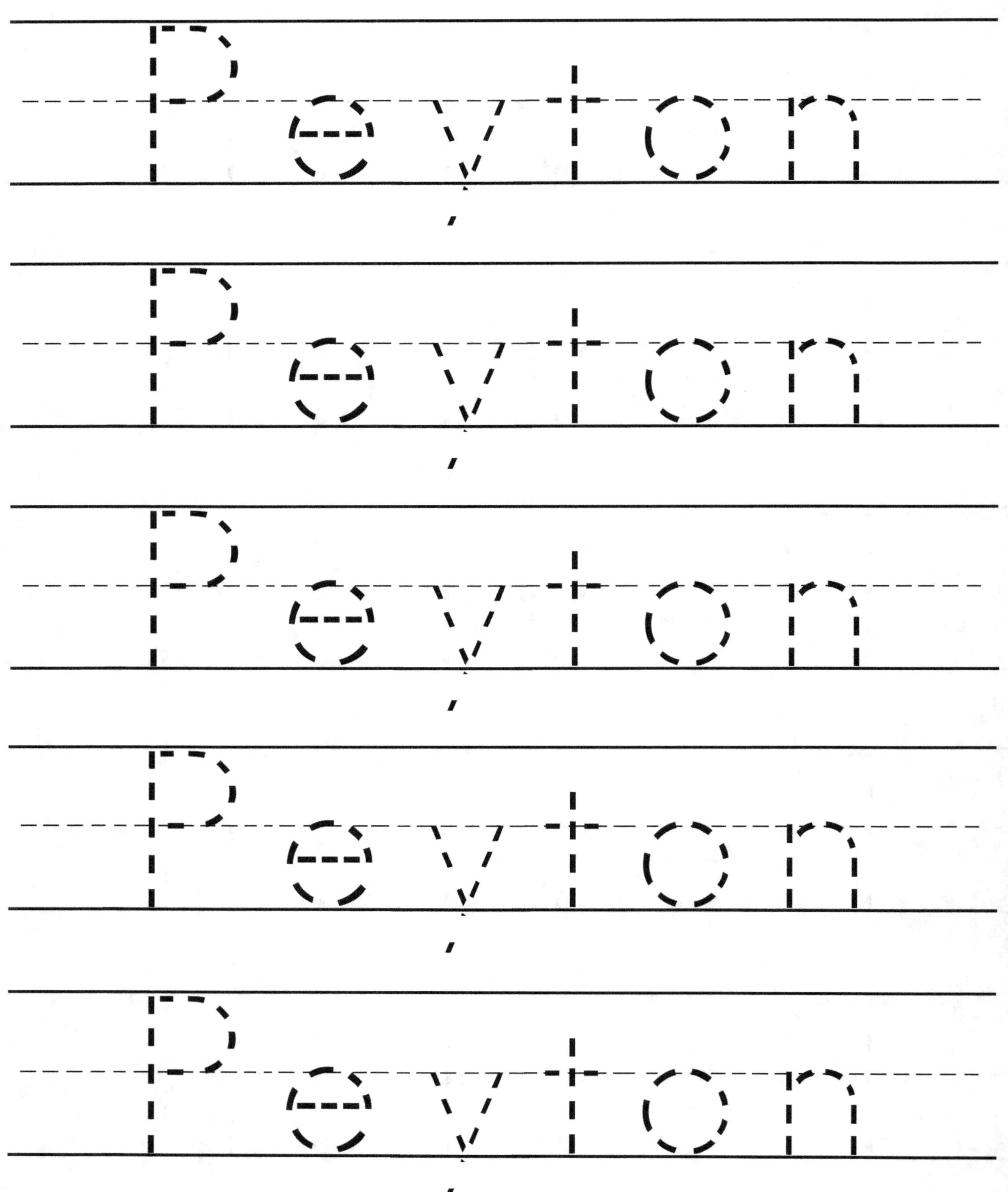

Peyton
Peyton
Peyton
Peyton
Peyton

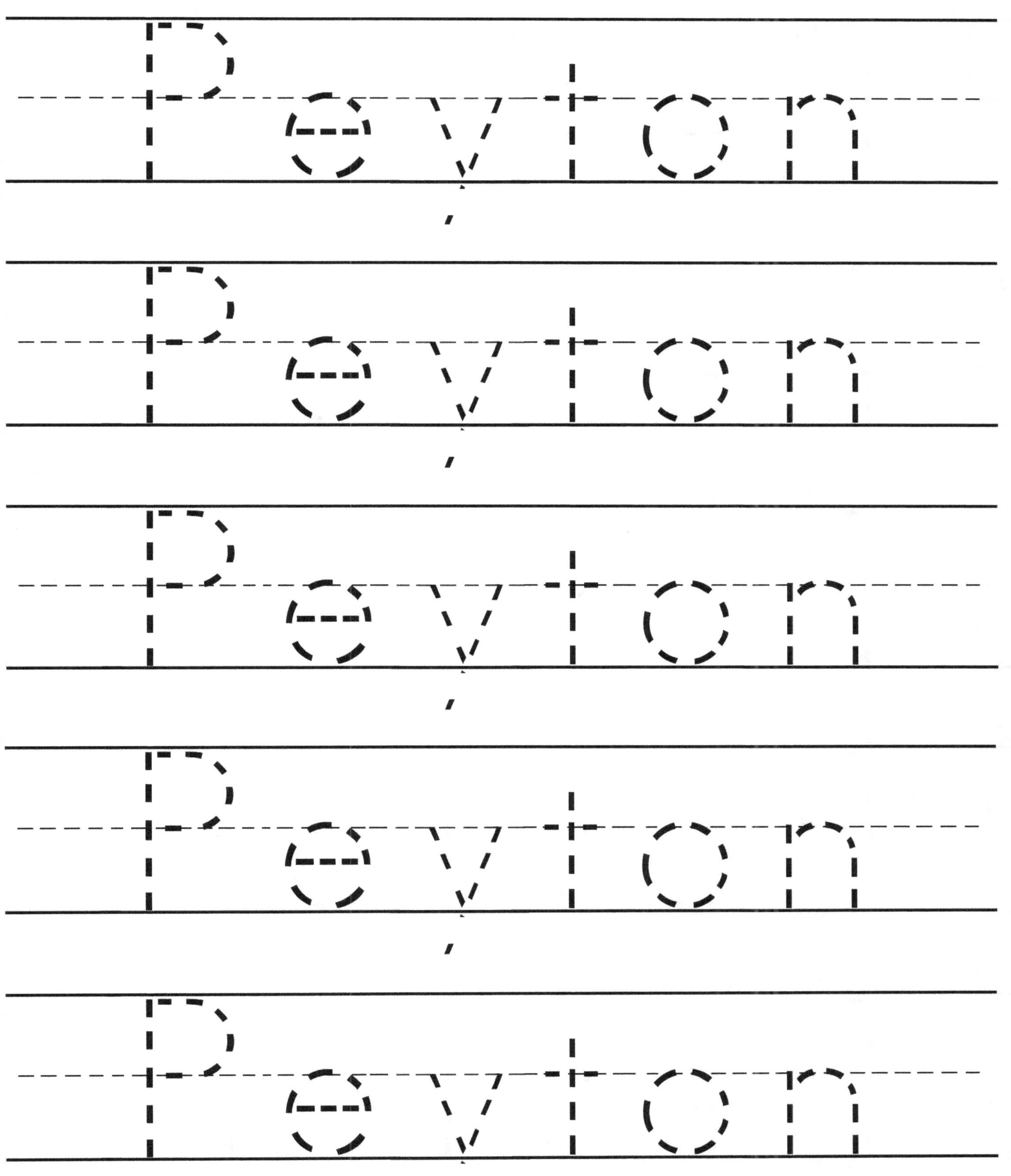

Peyton
Peyton
Peyton
Peyton
Peyton

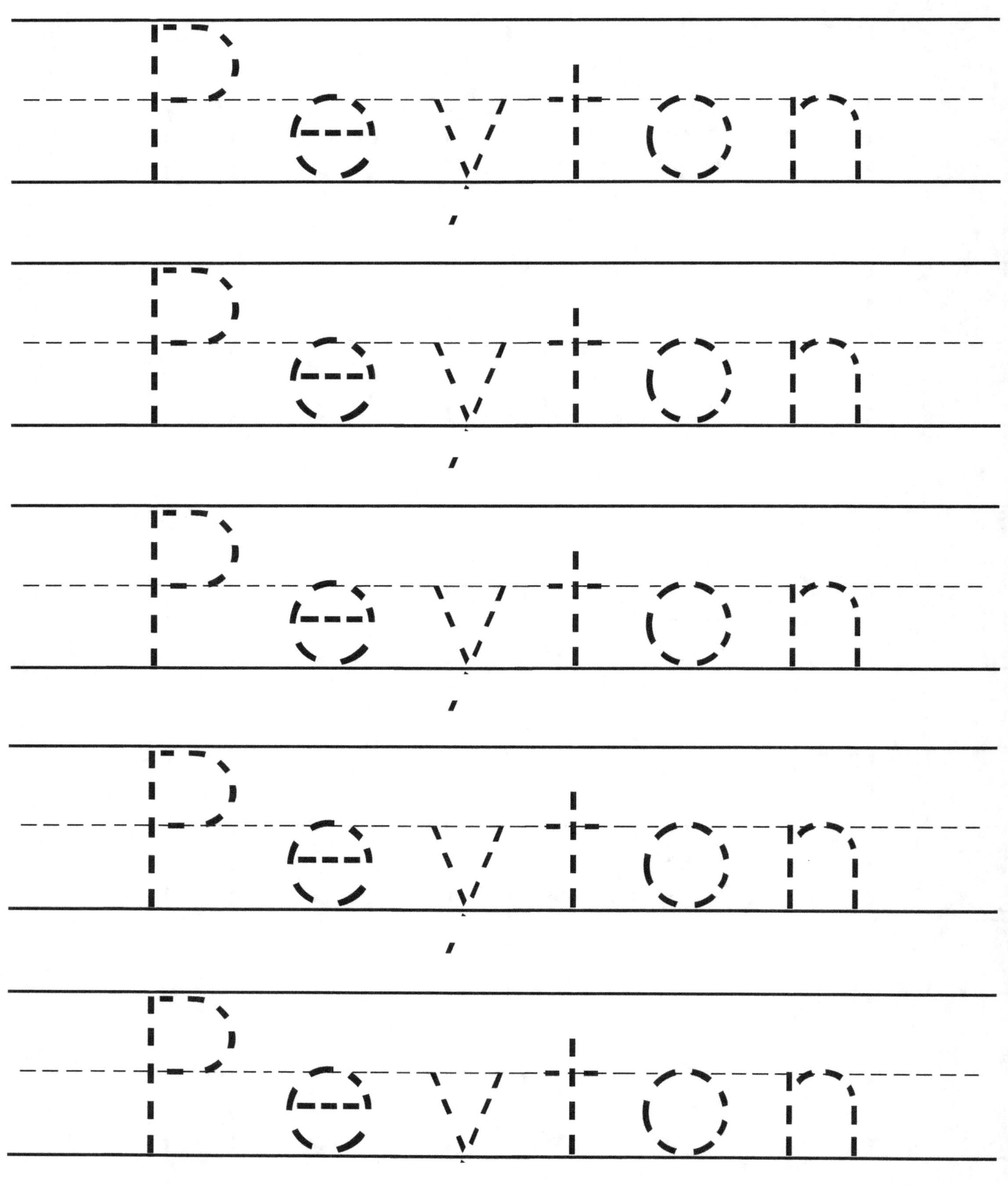

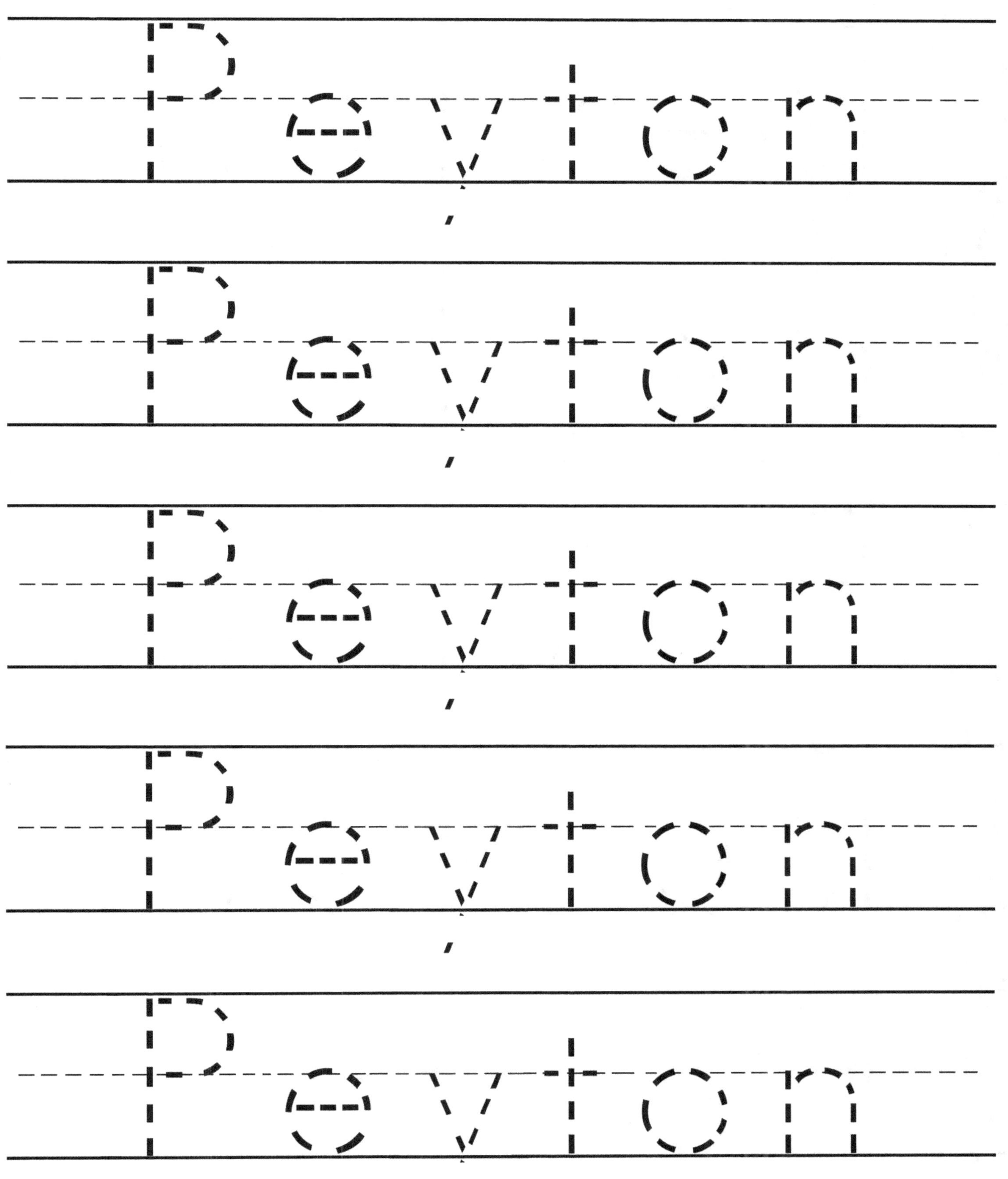

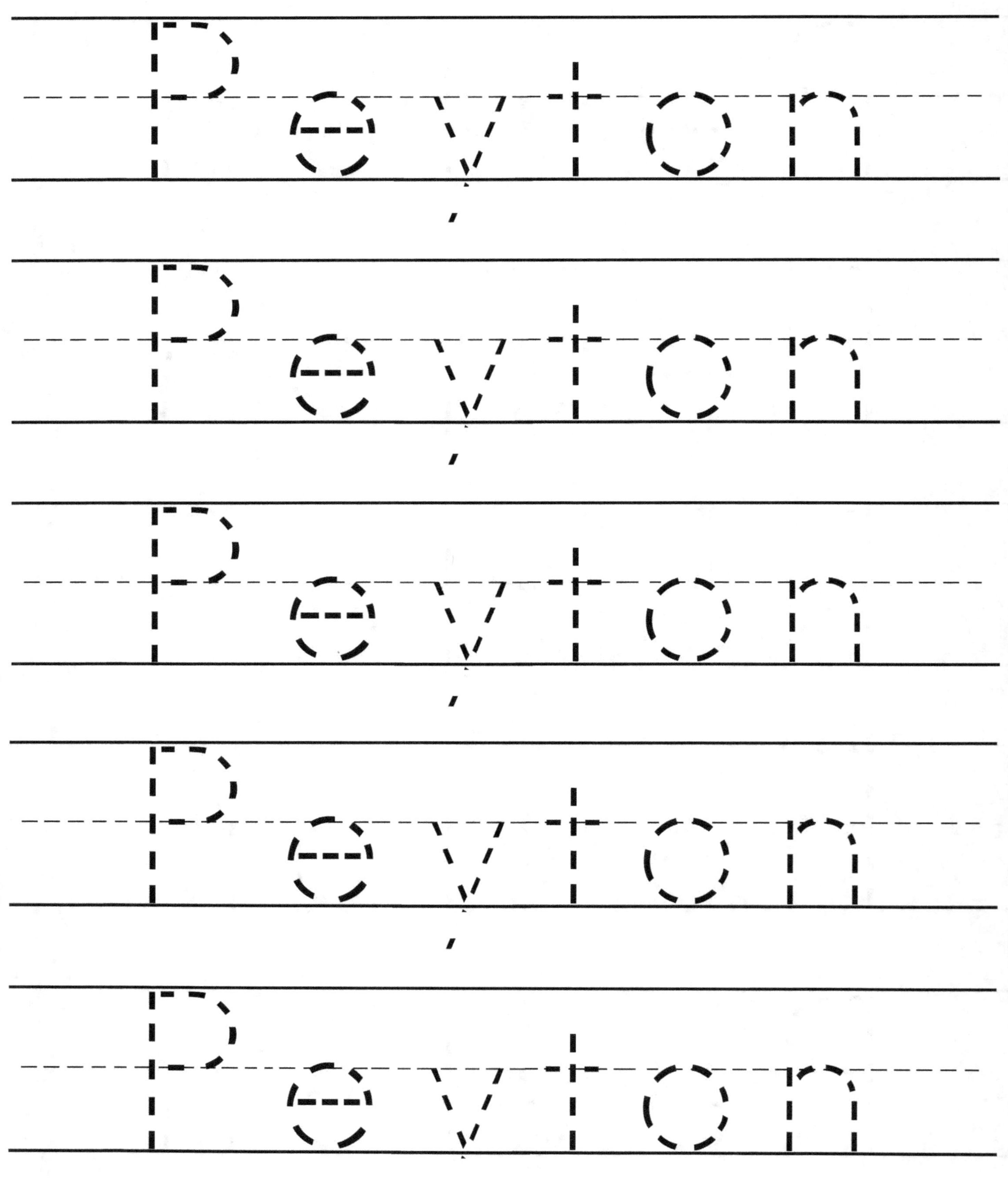

Peyton
Peyton
Peyton
Peyton
Peyton

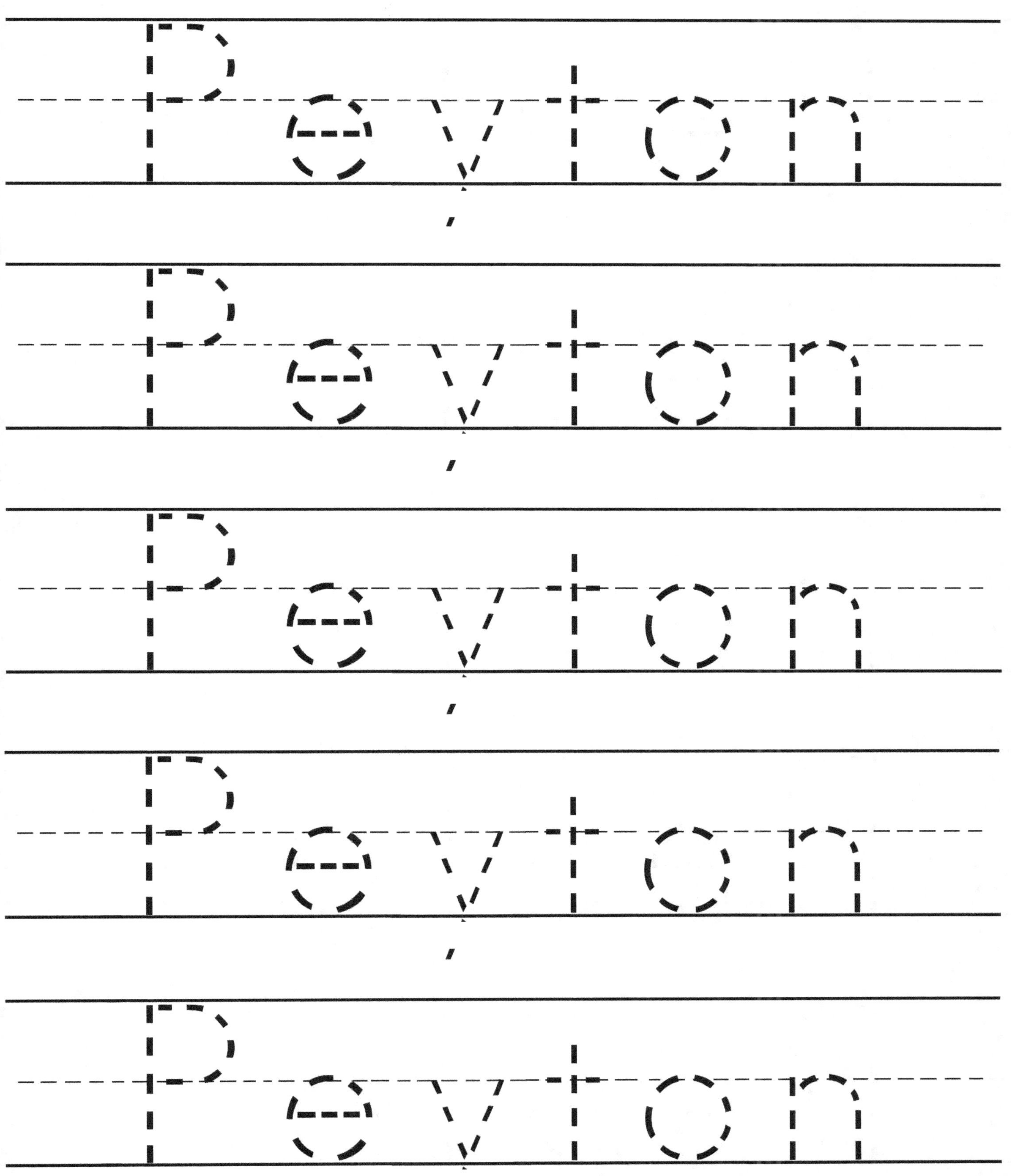

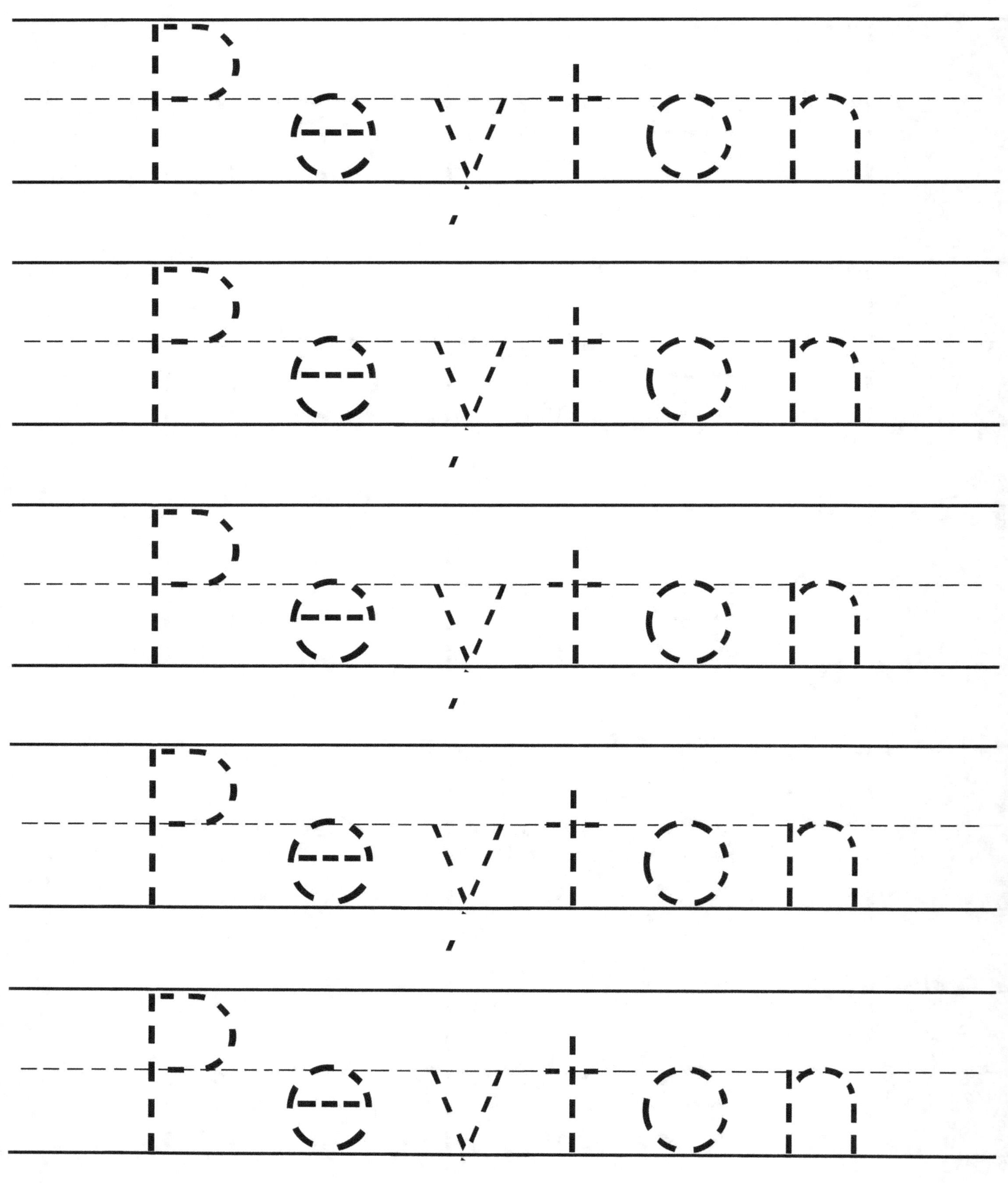
Peyton
Peyton
Peyton
Peyton
Peyton

P P P P

P P P P

P P P P

P P P P

P P P P

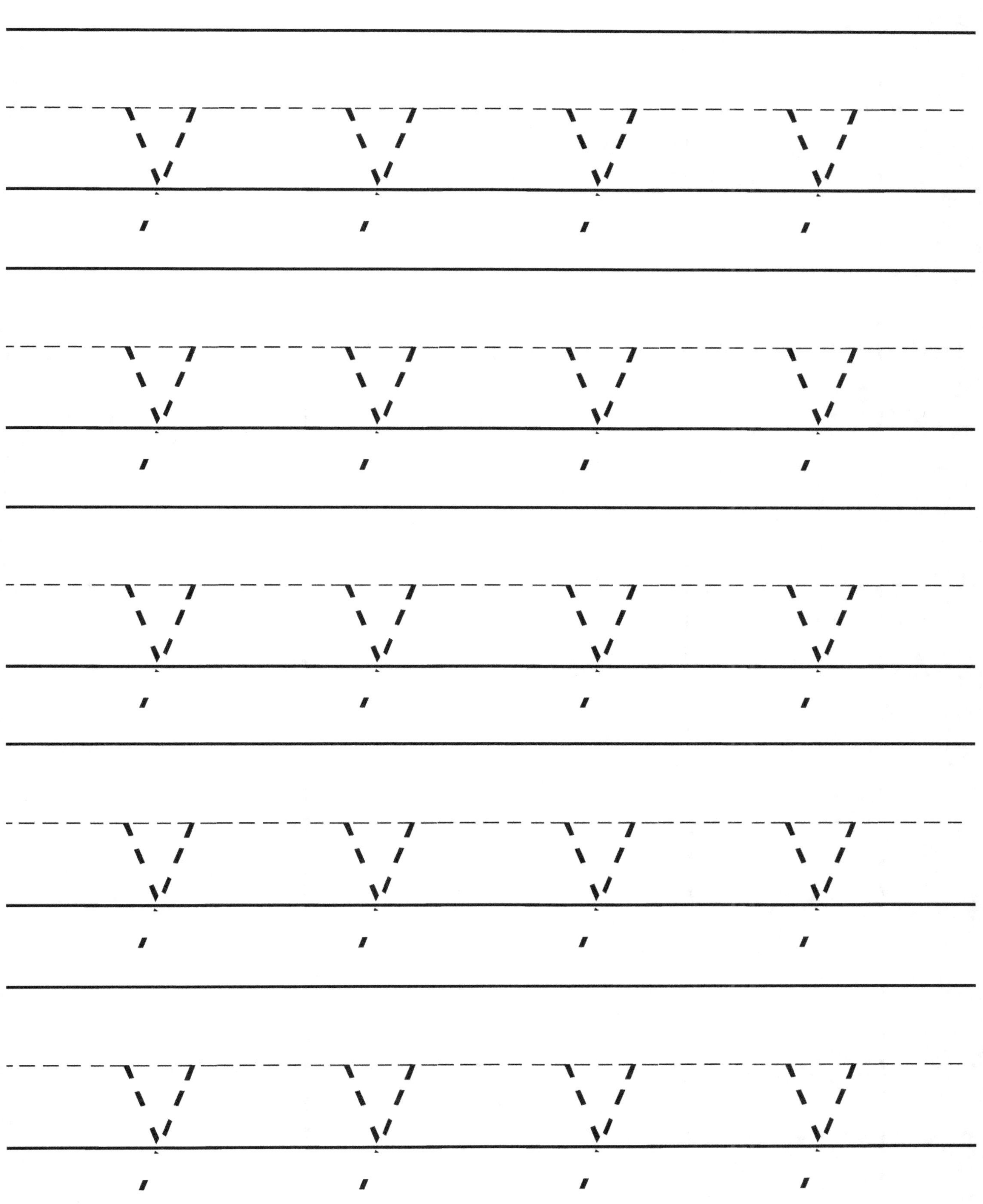

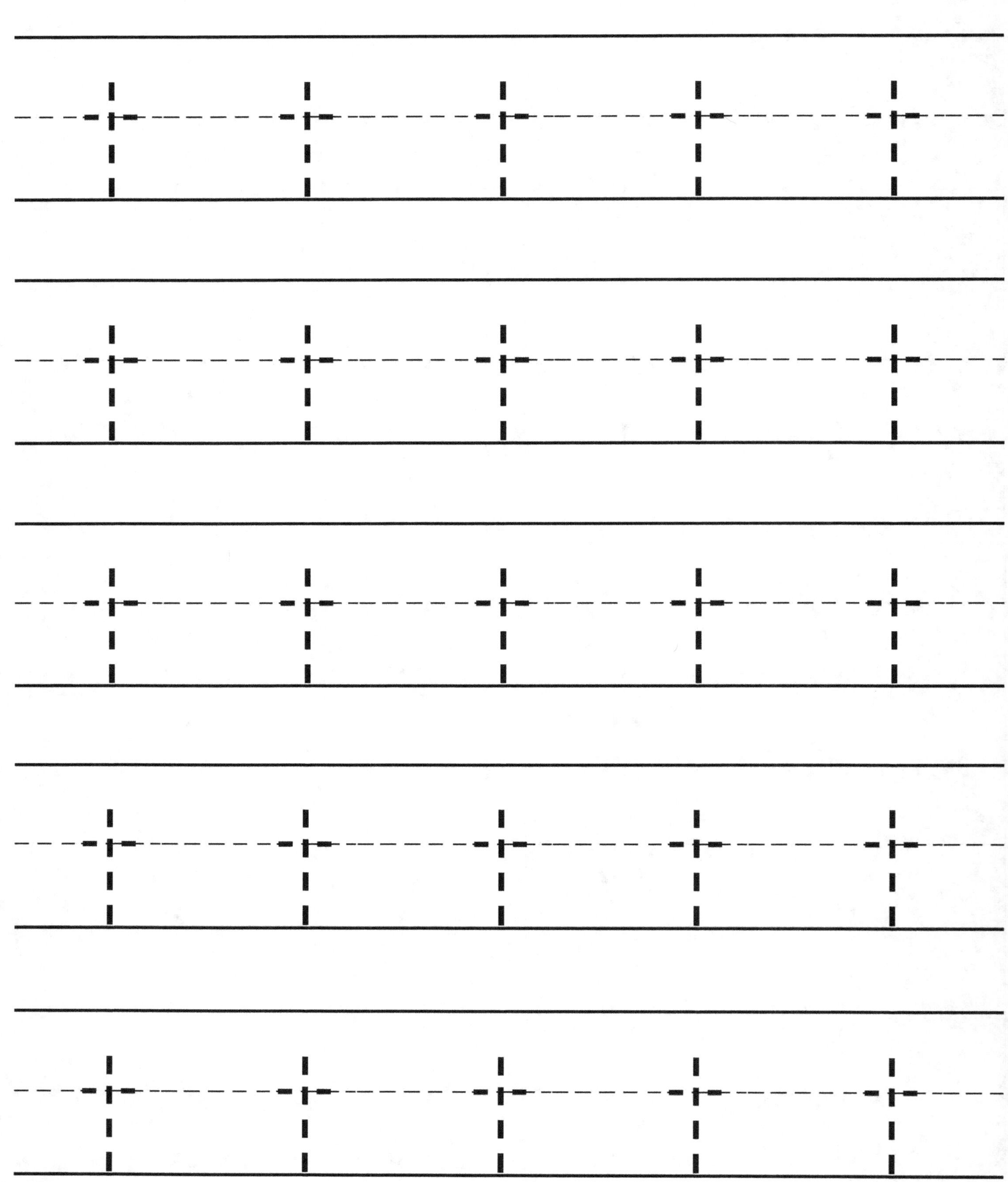

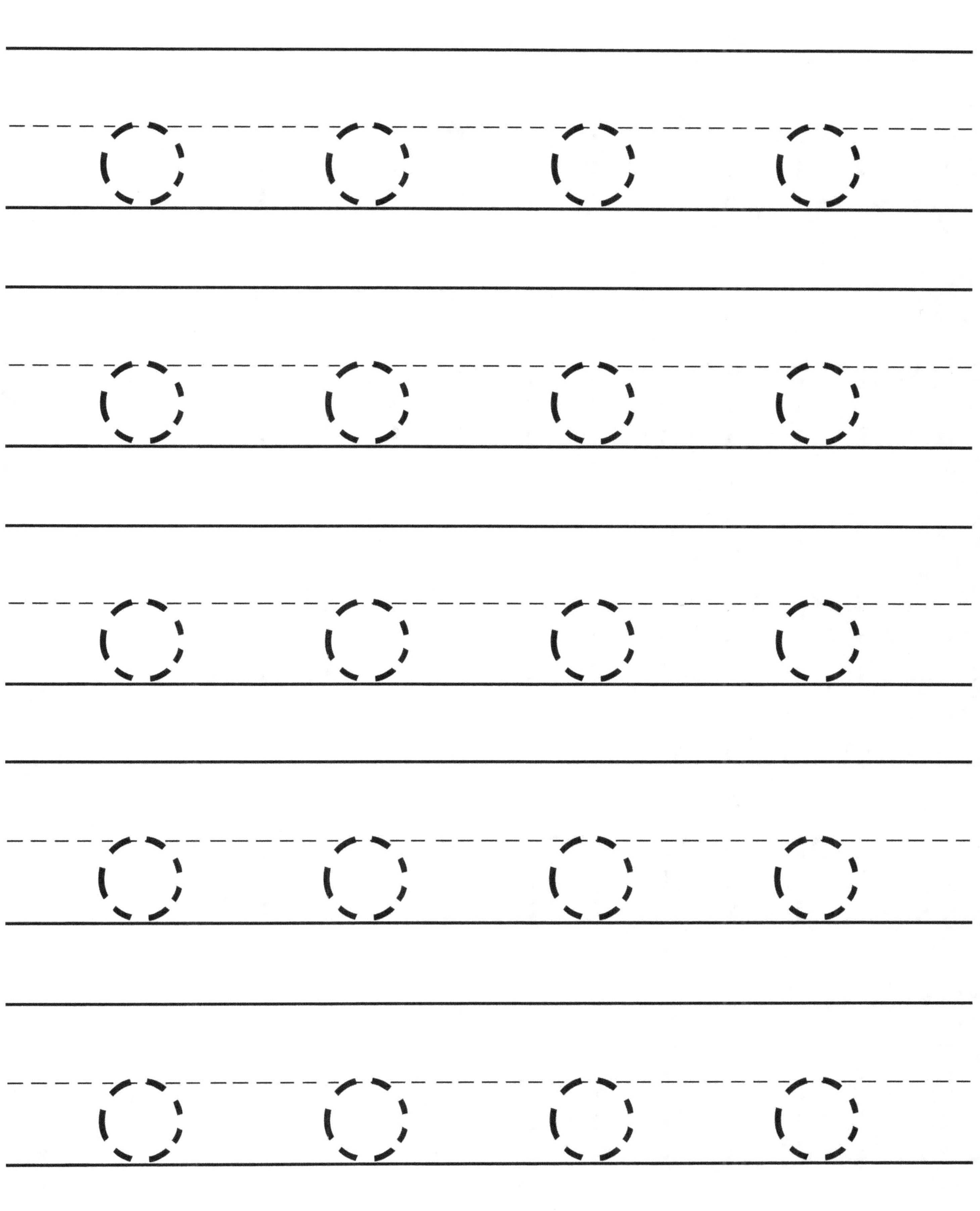

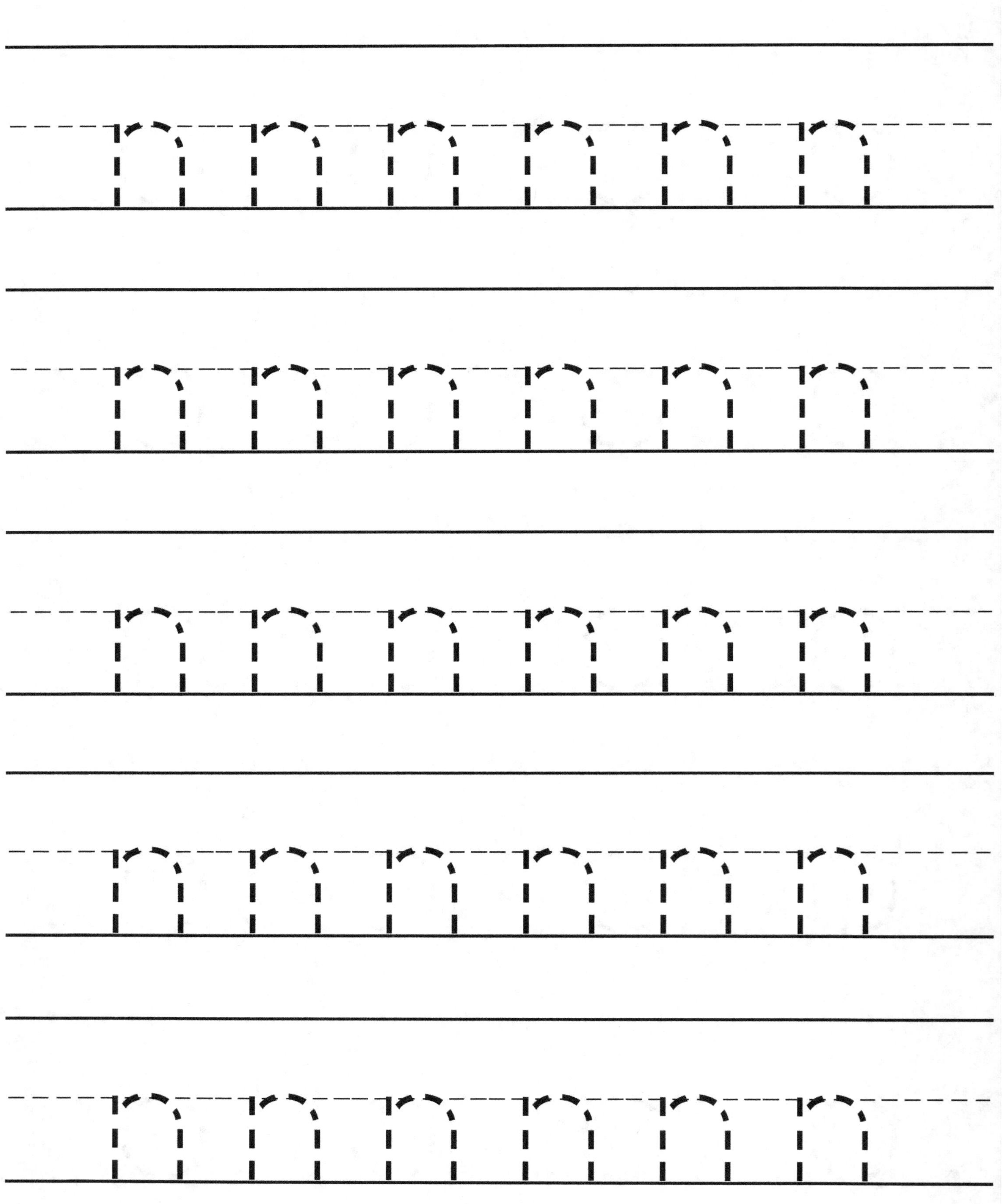

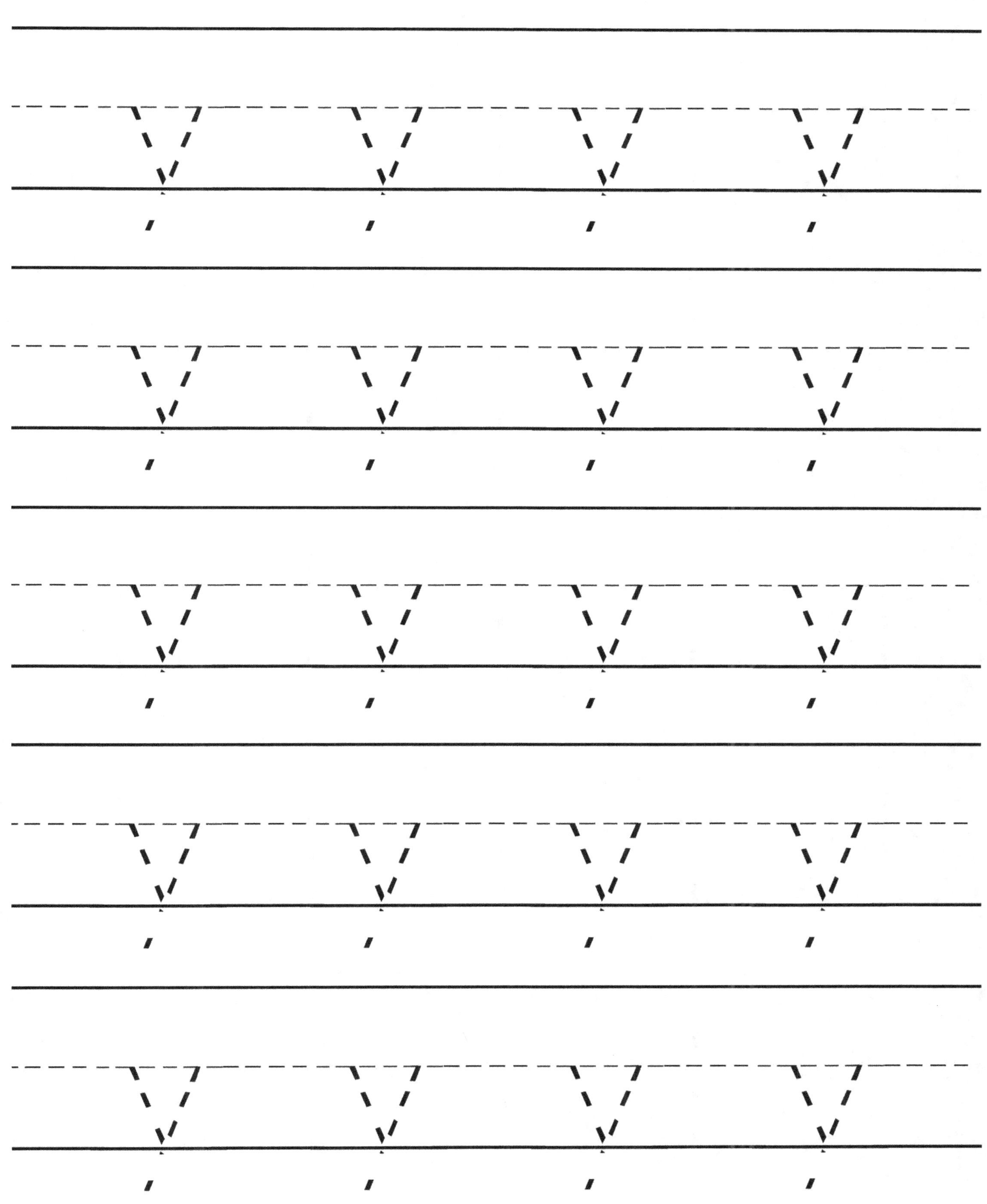

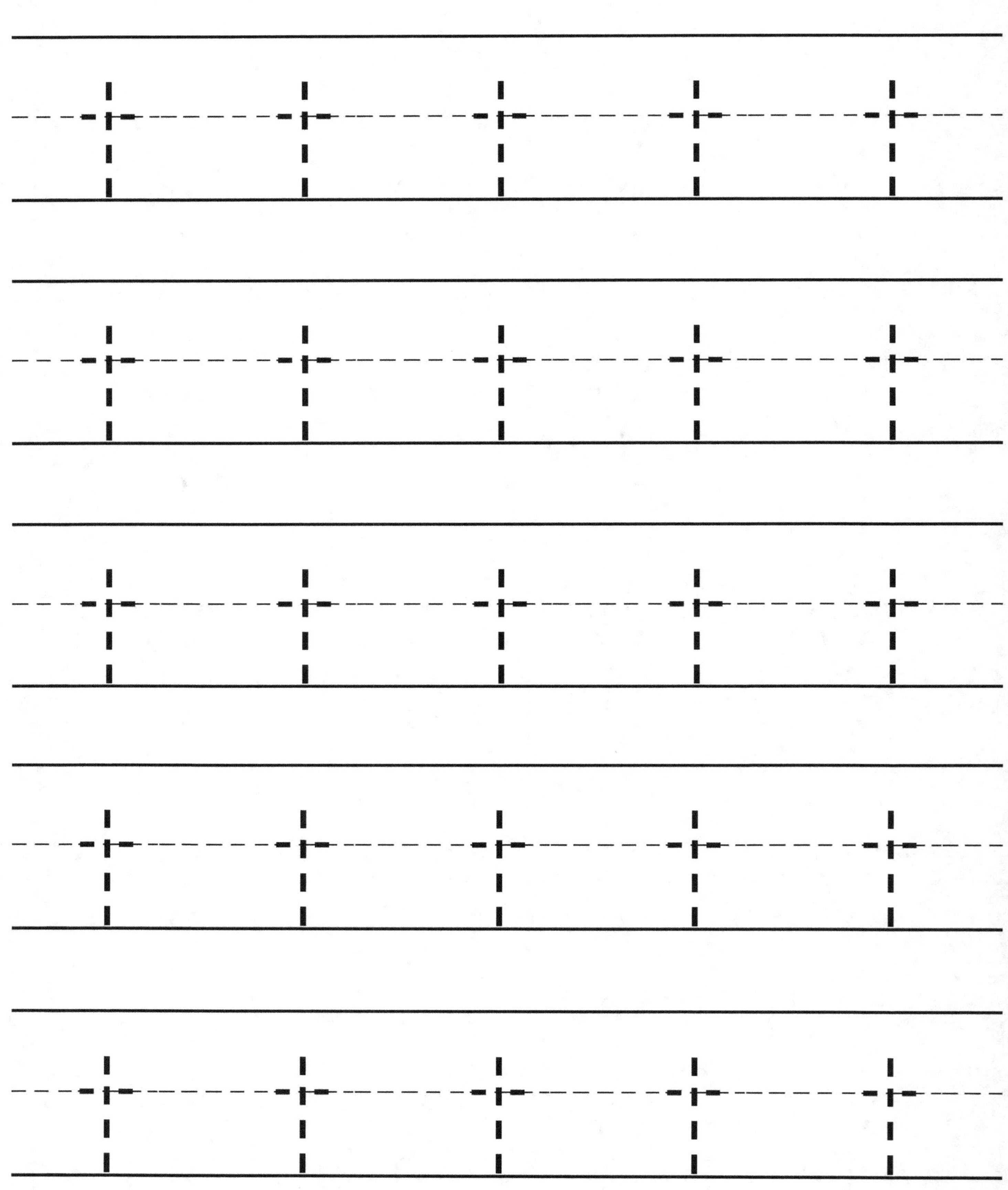

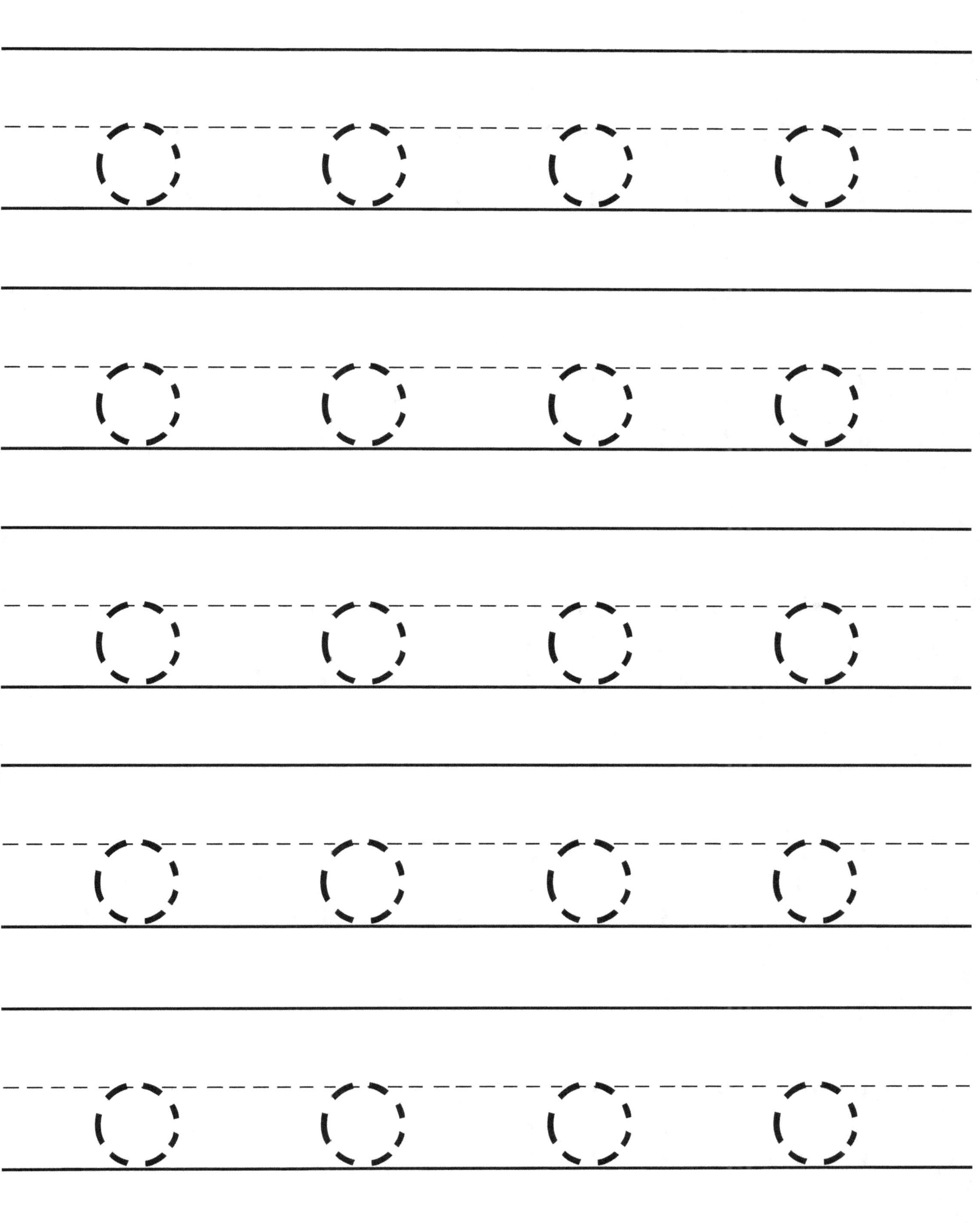

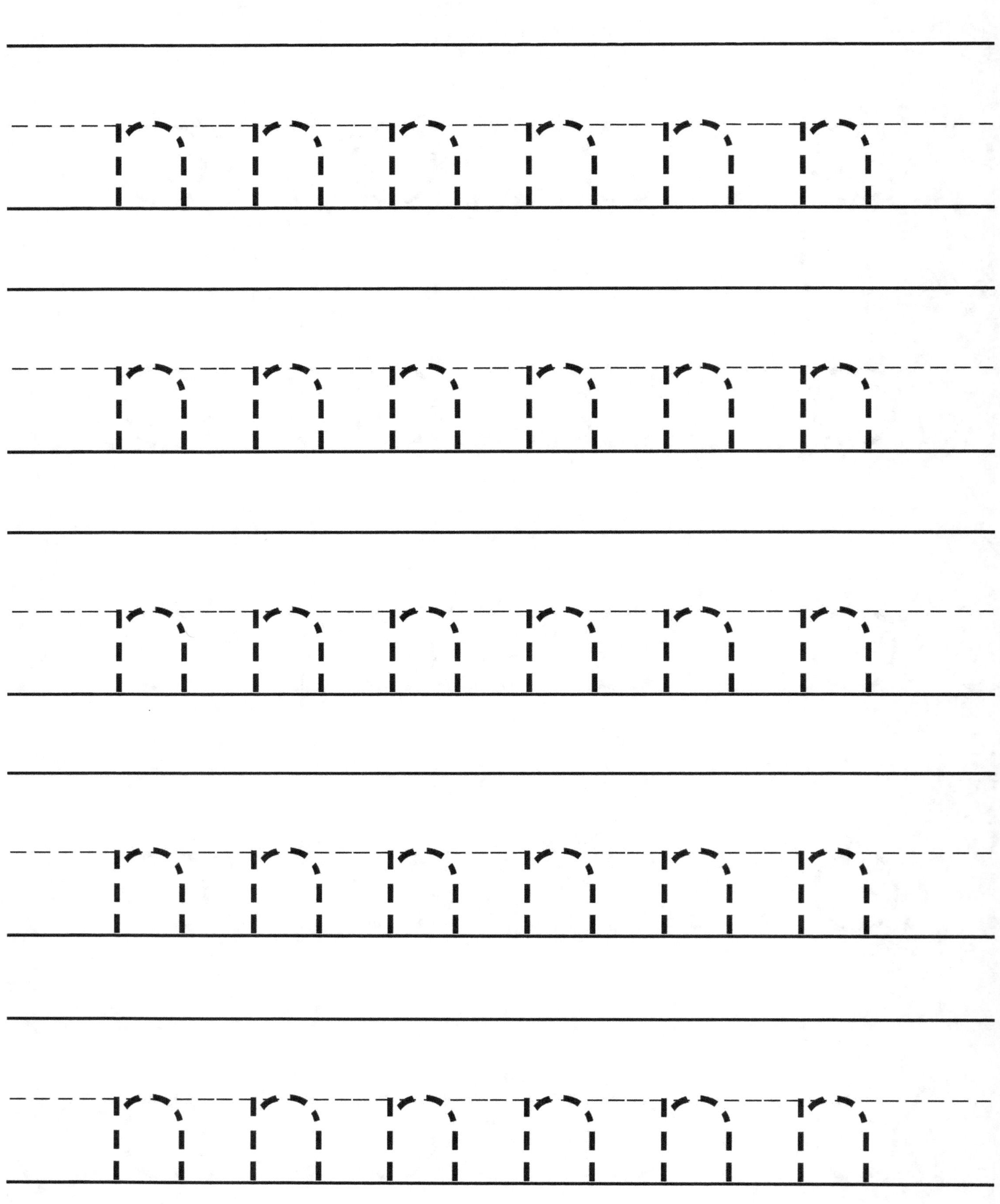

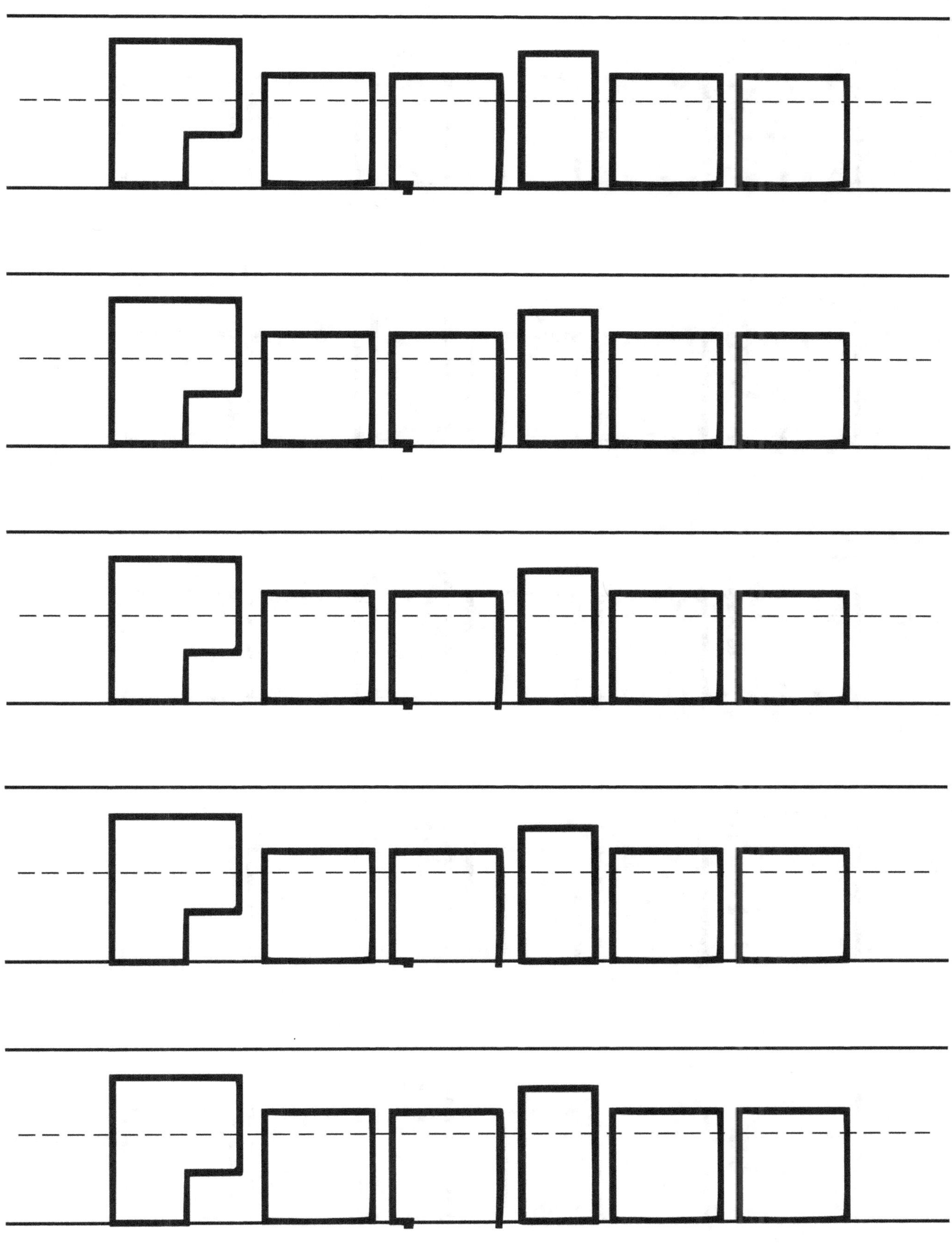

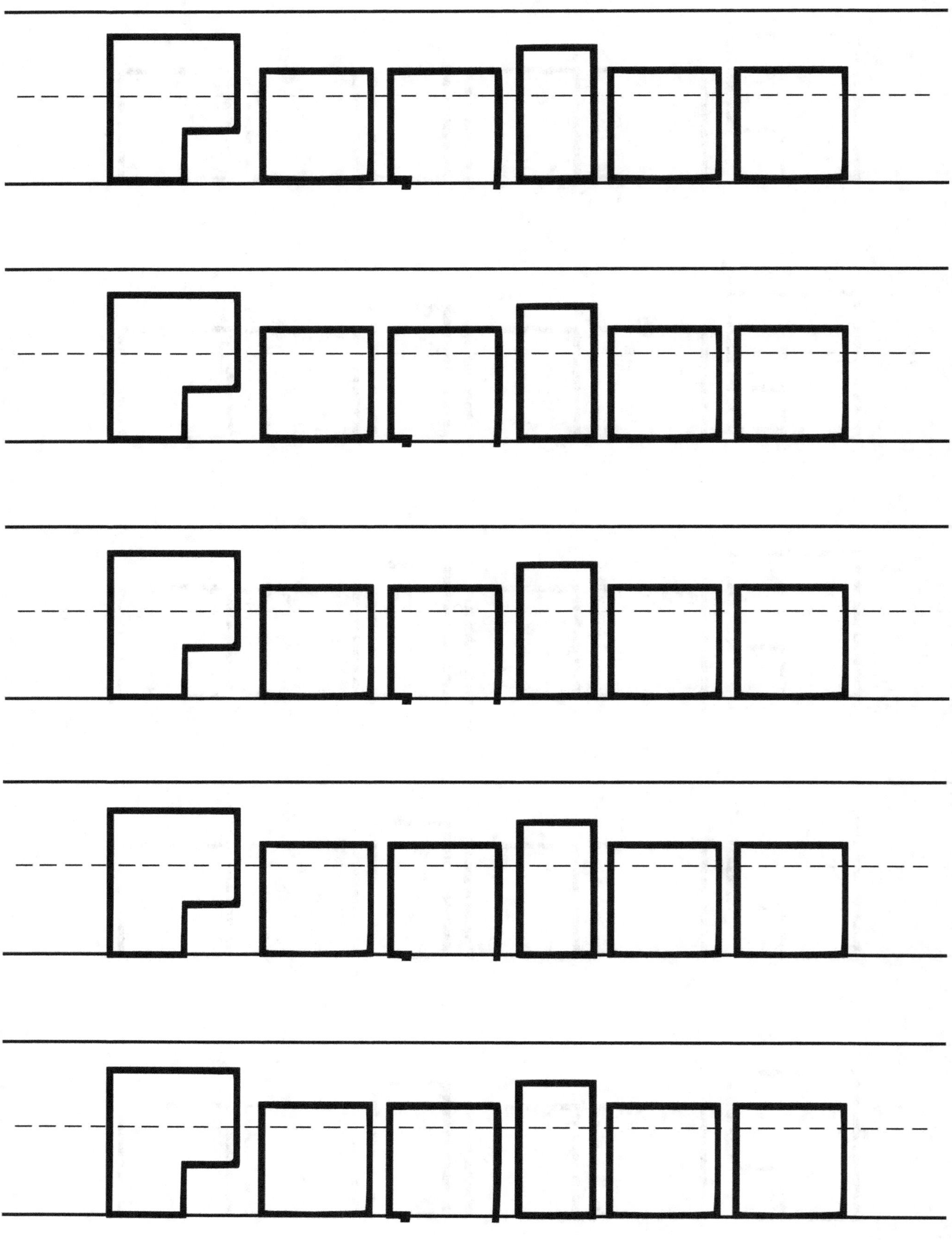

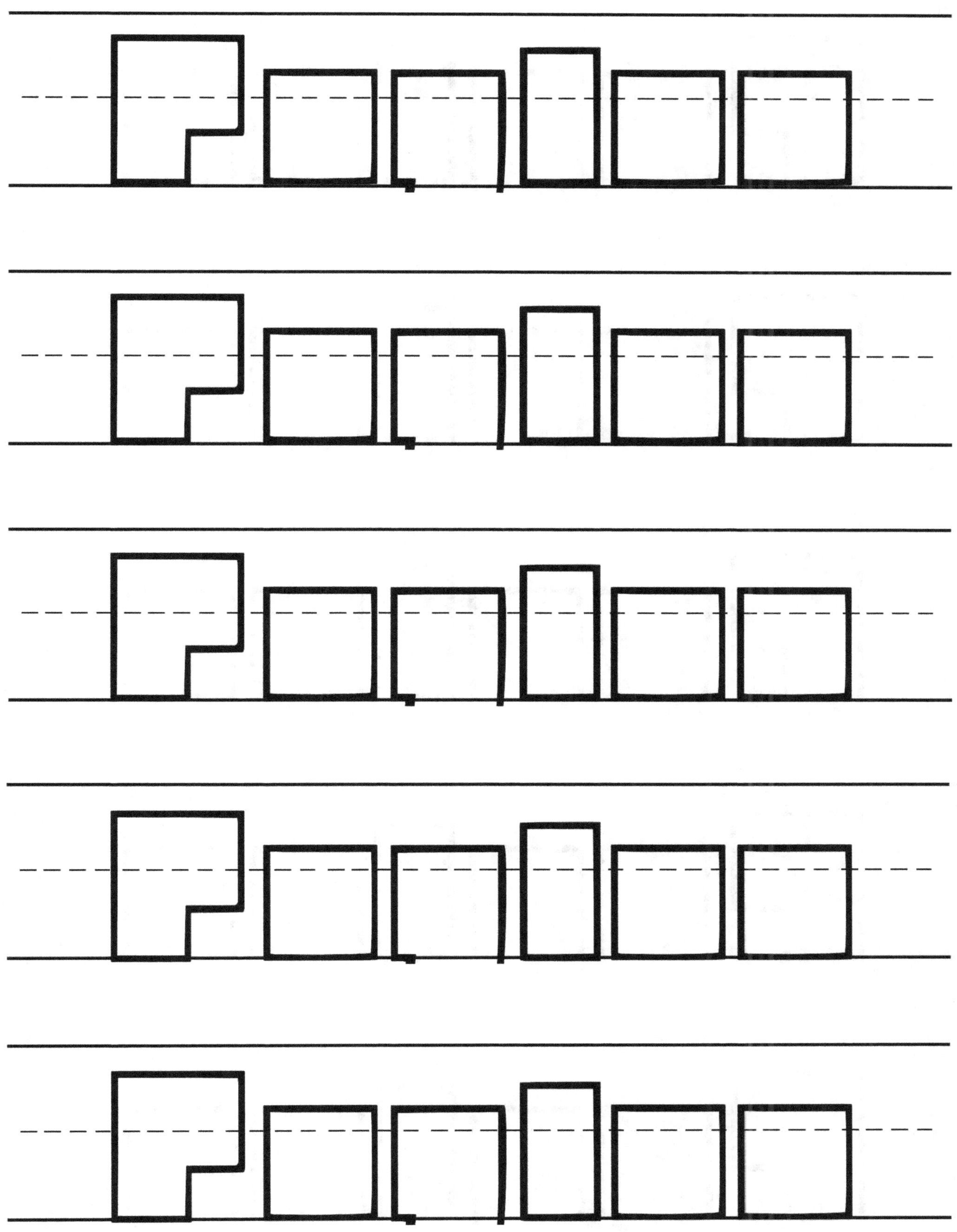

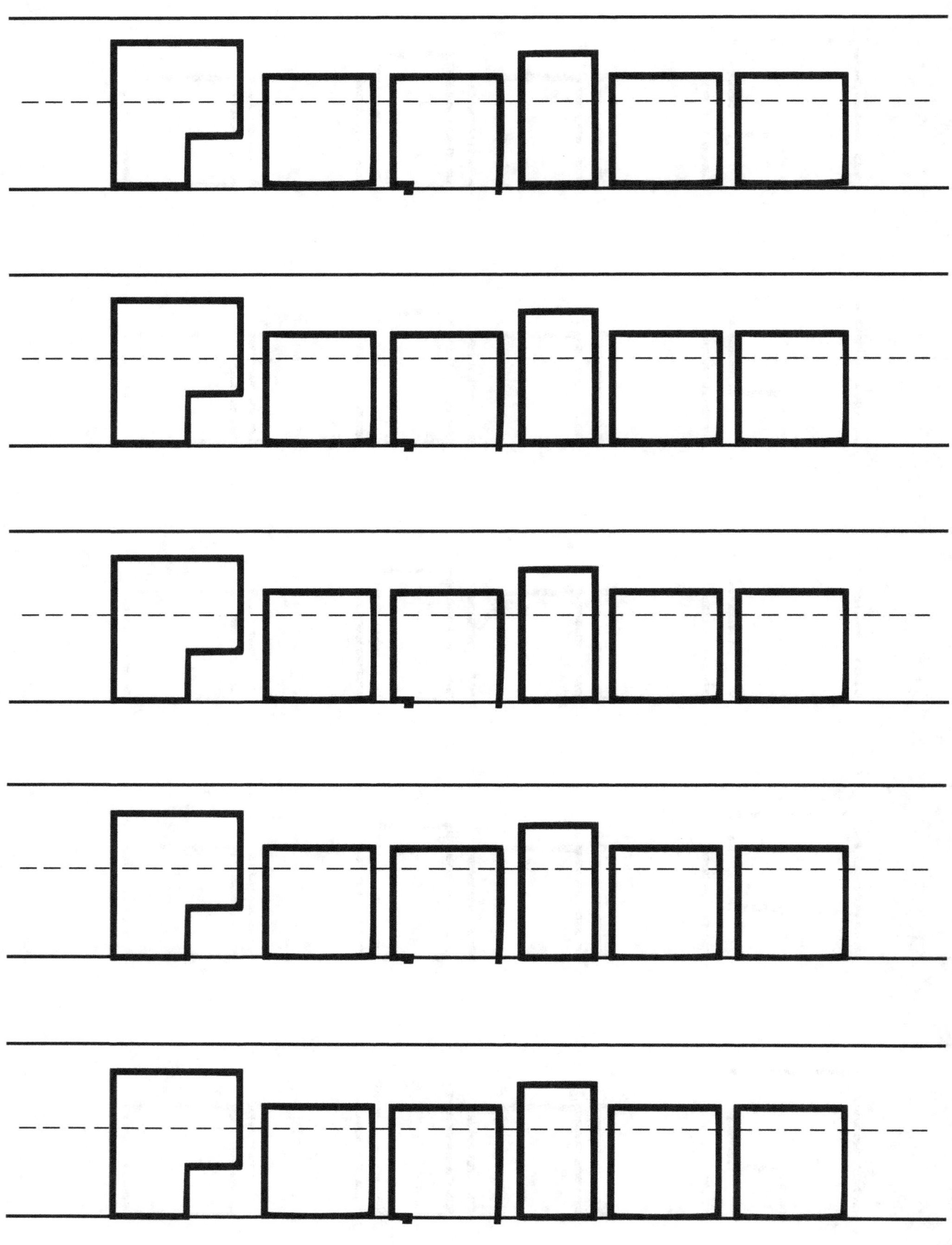

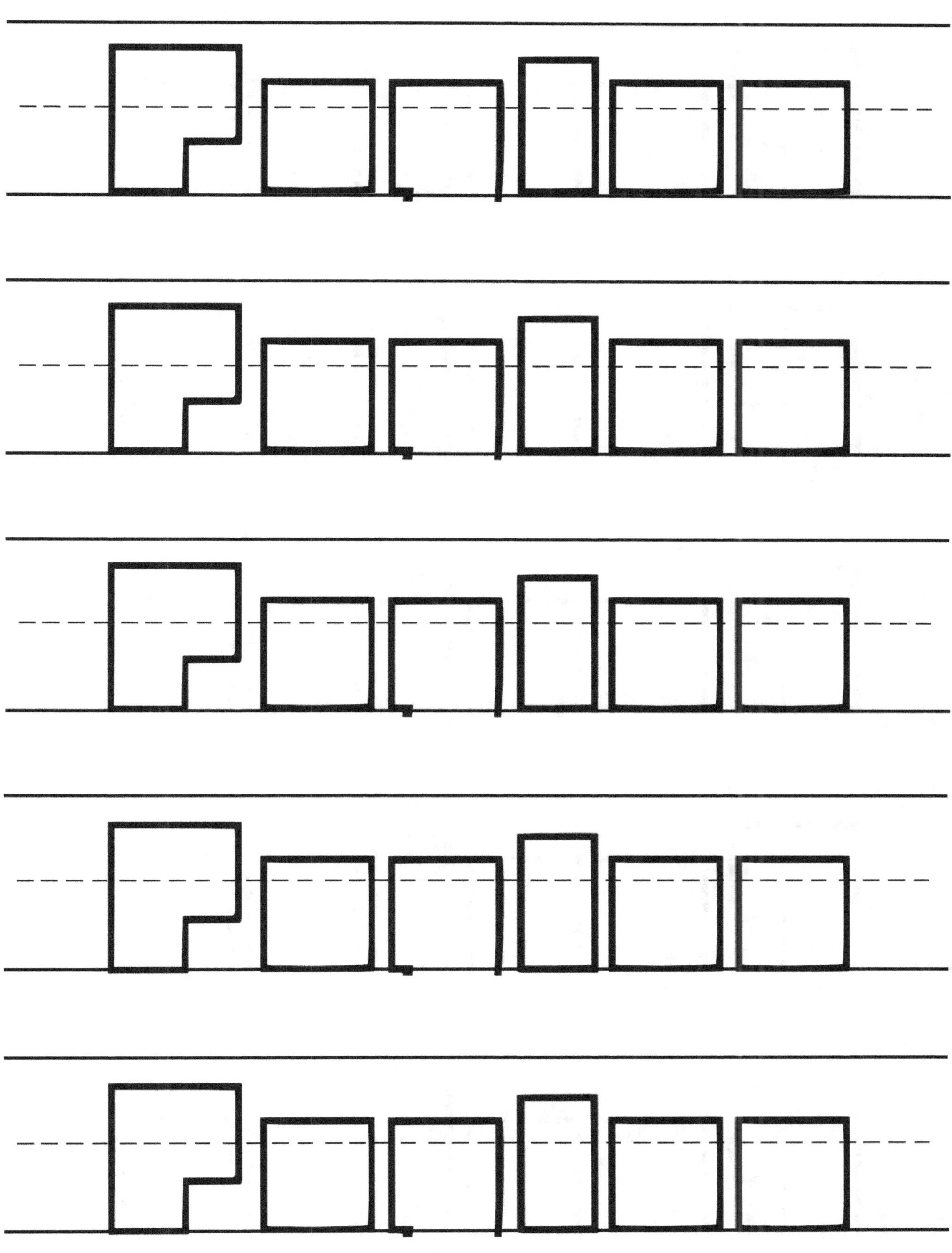

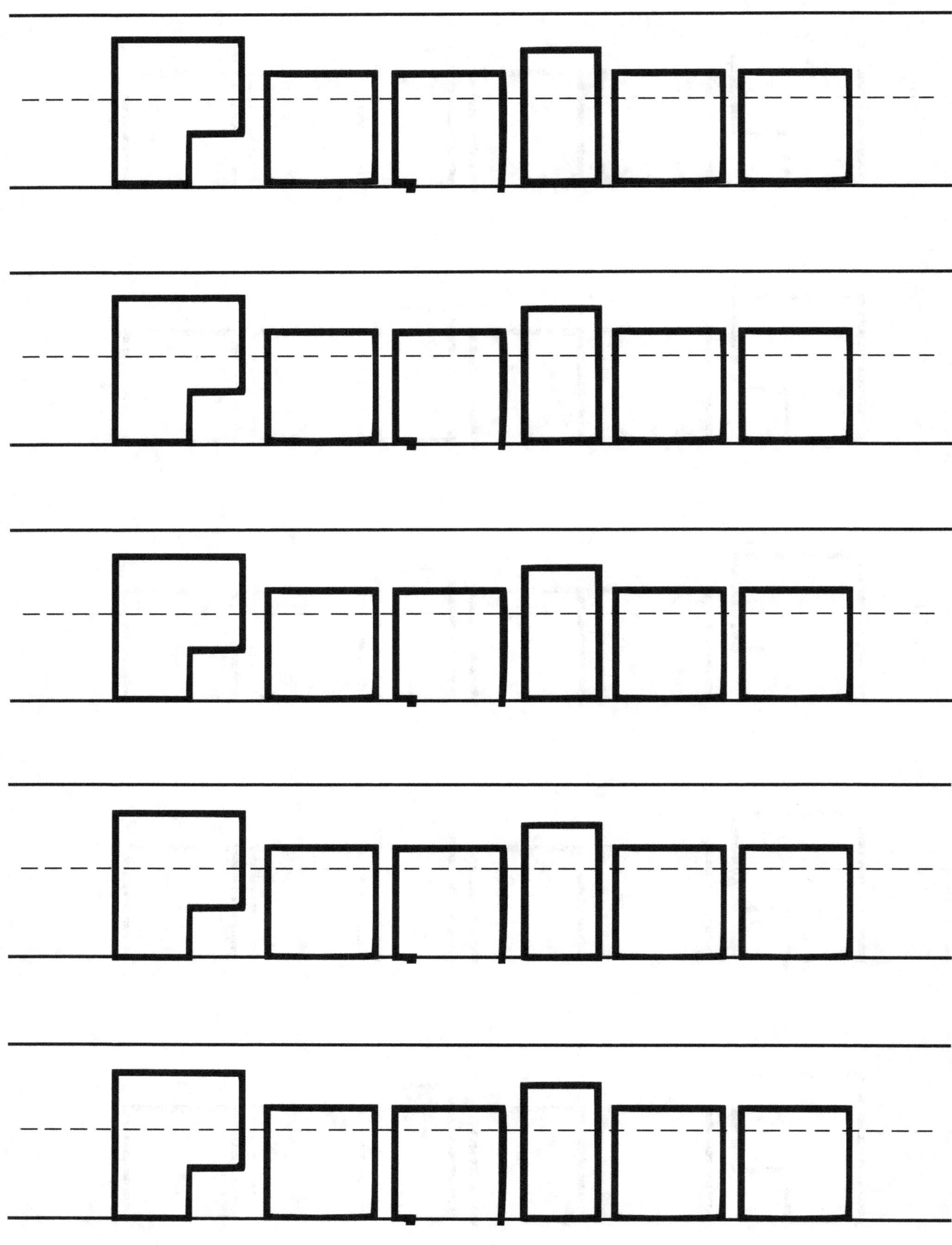

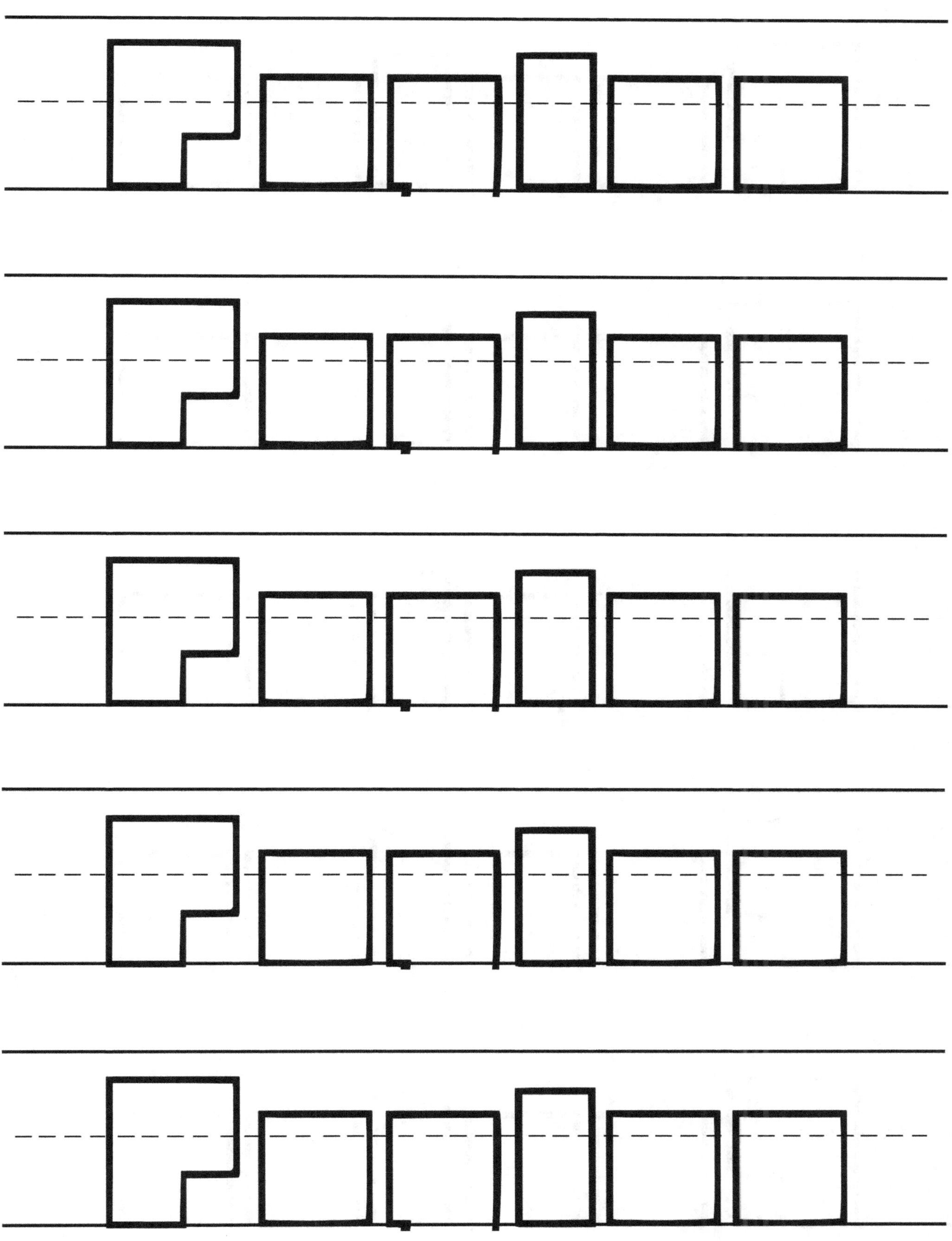

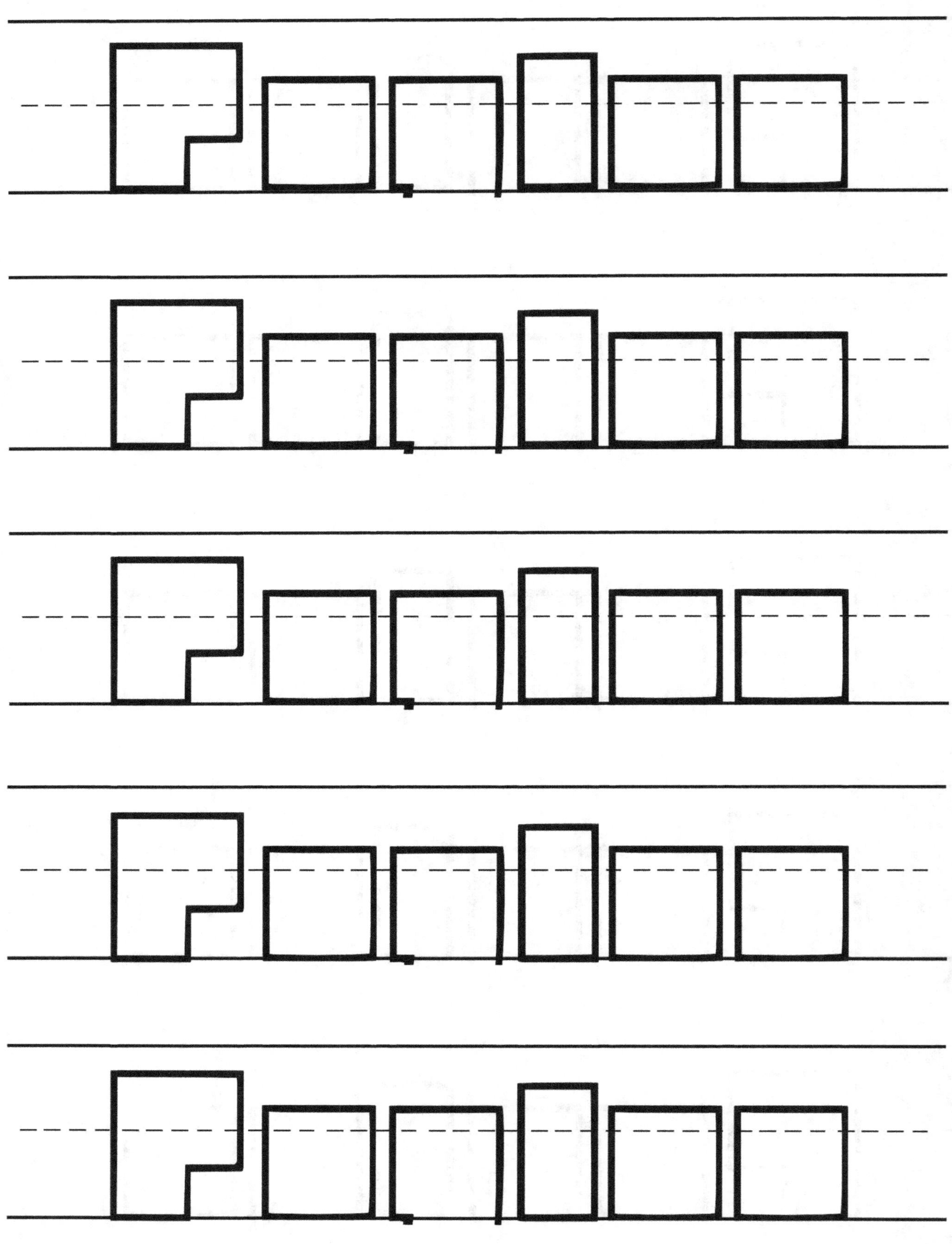

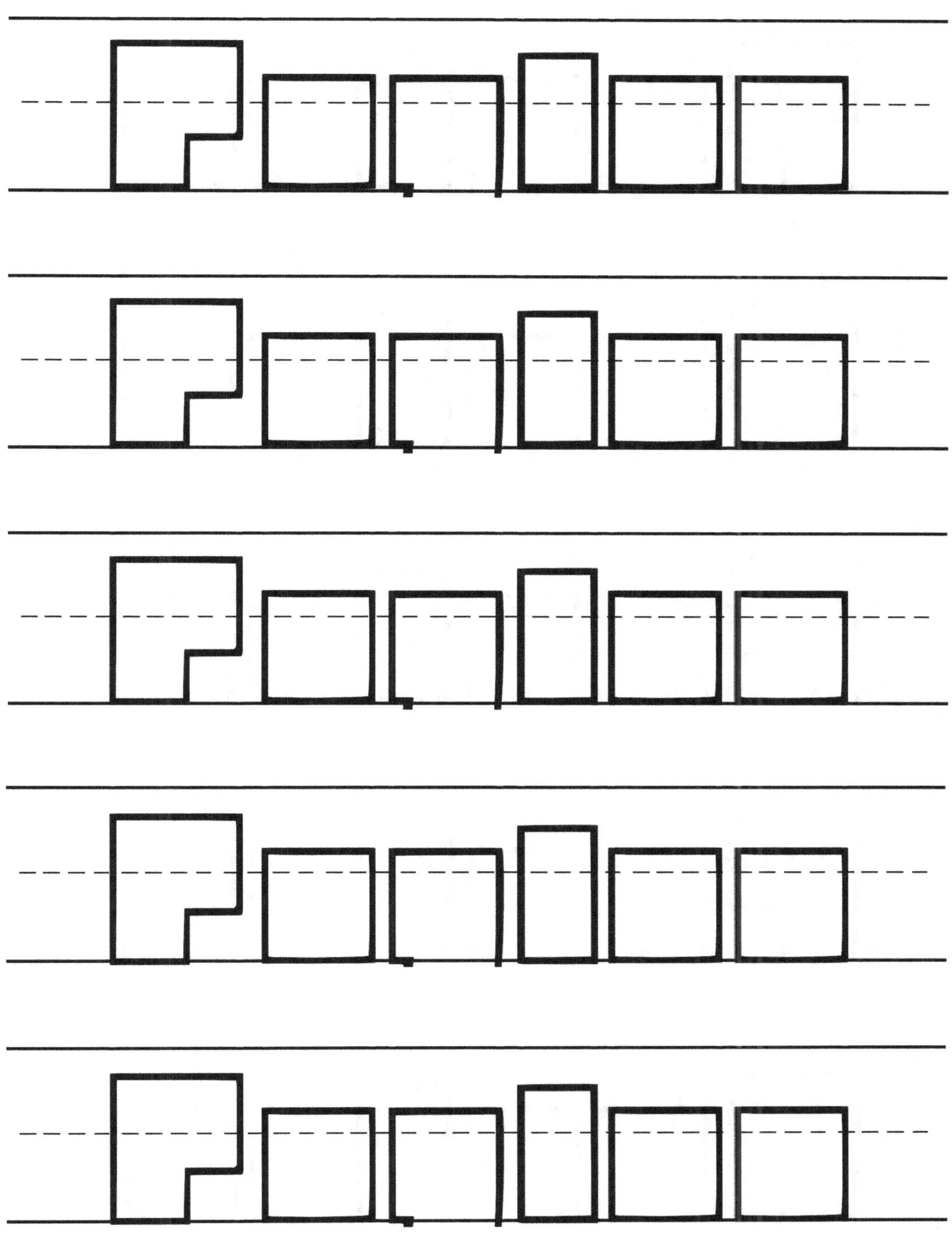

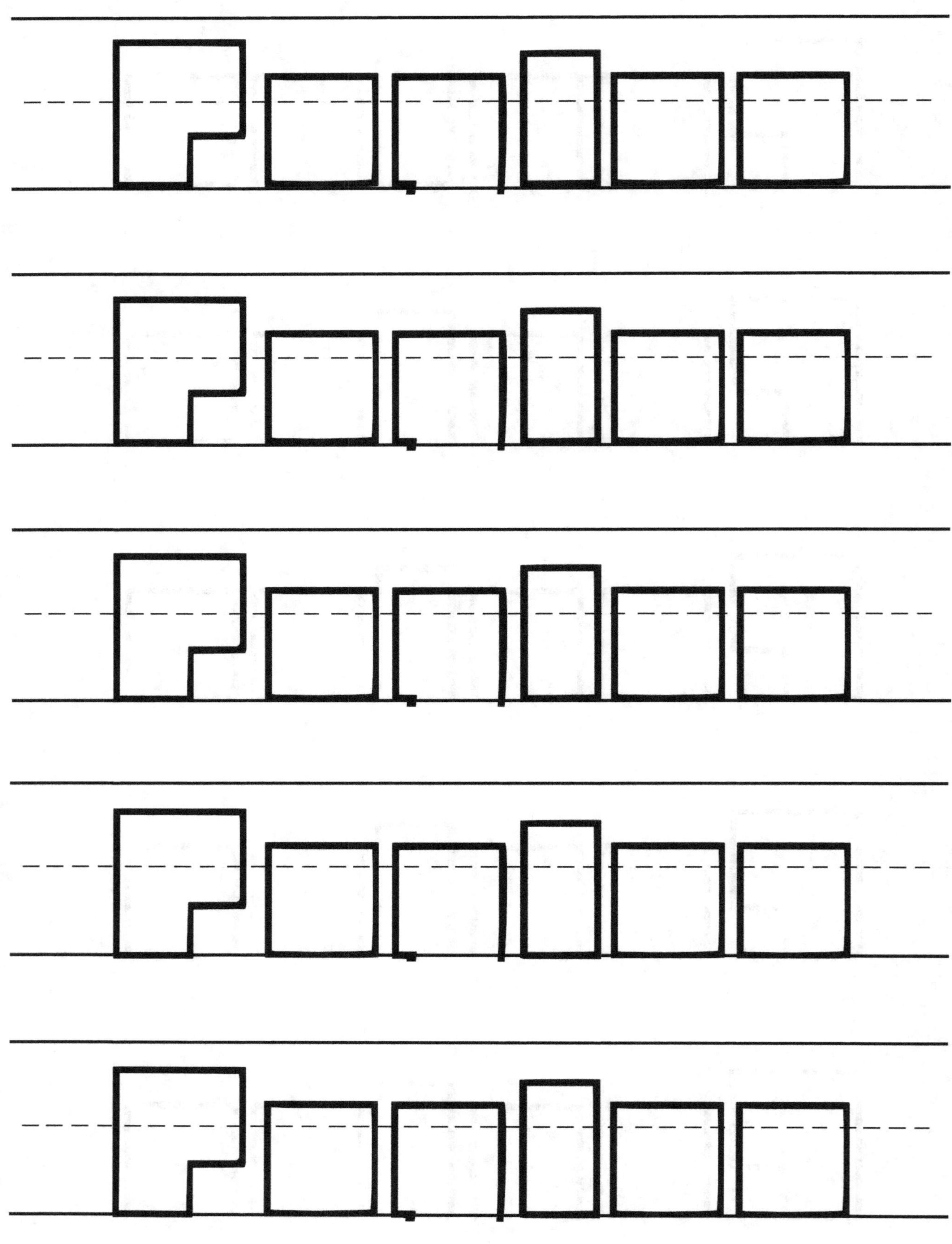

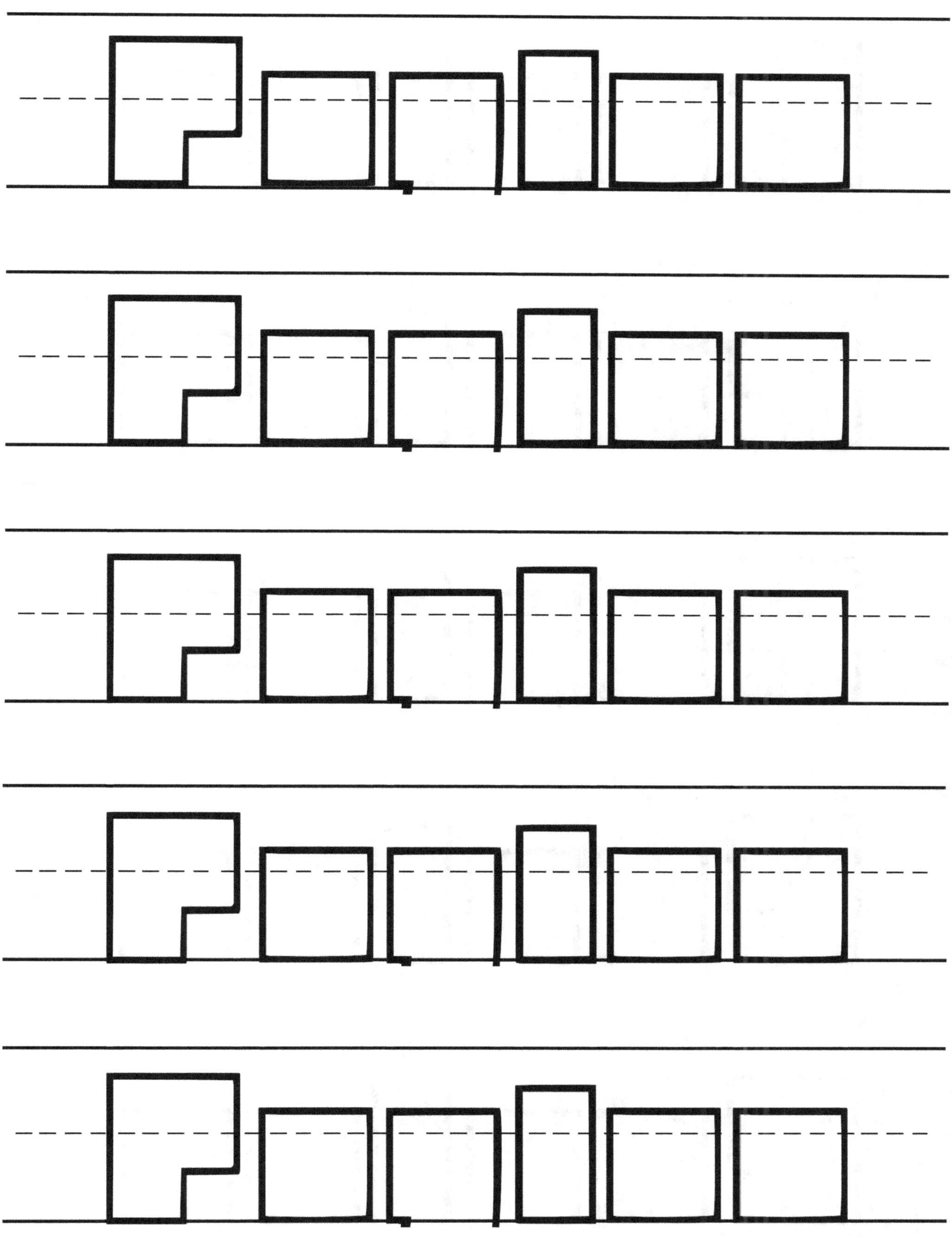

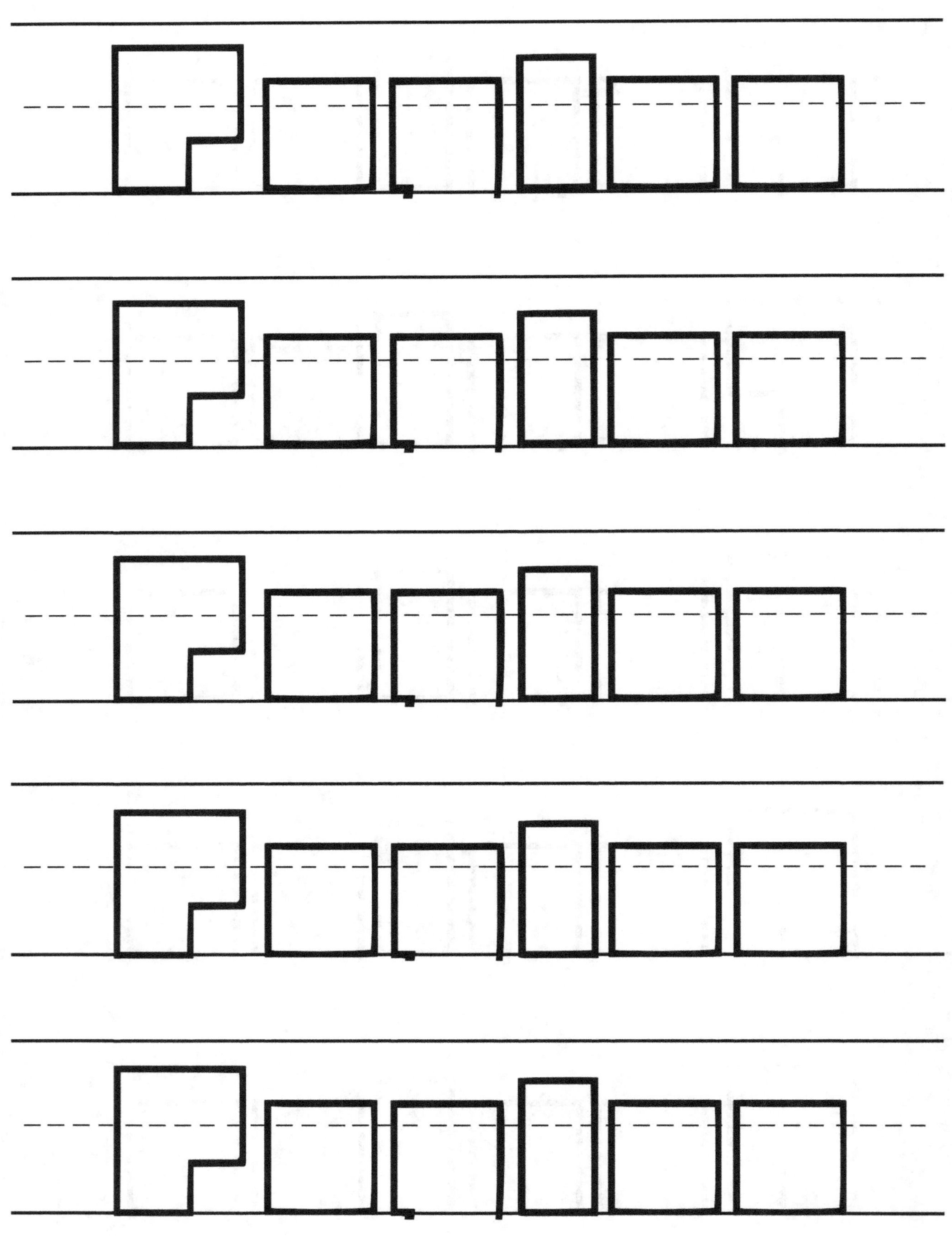

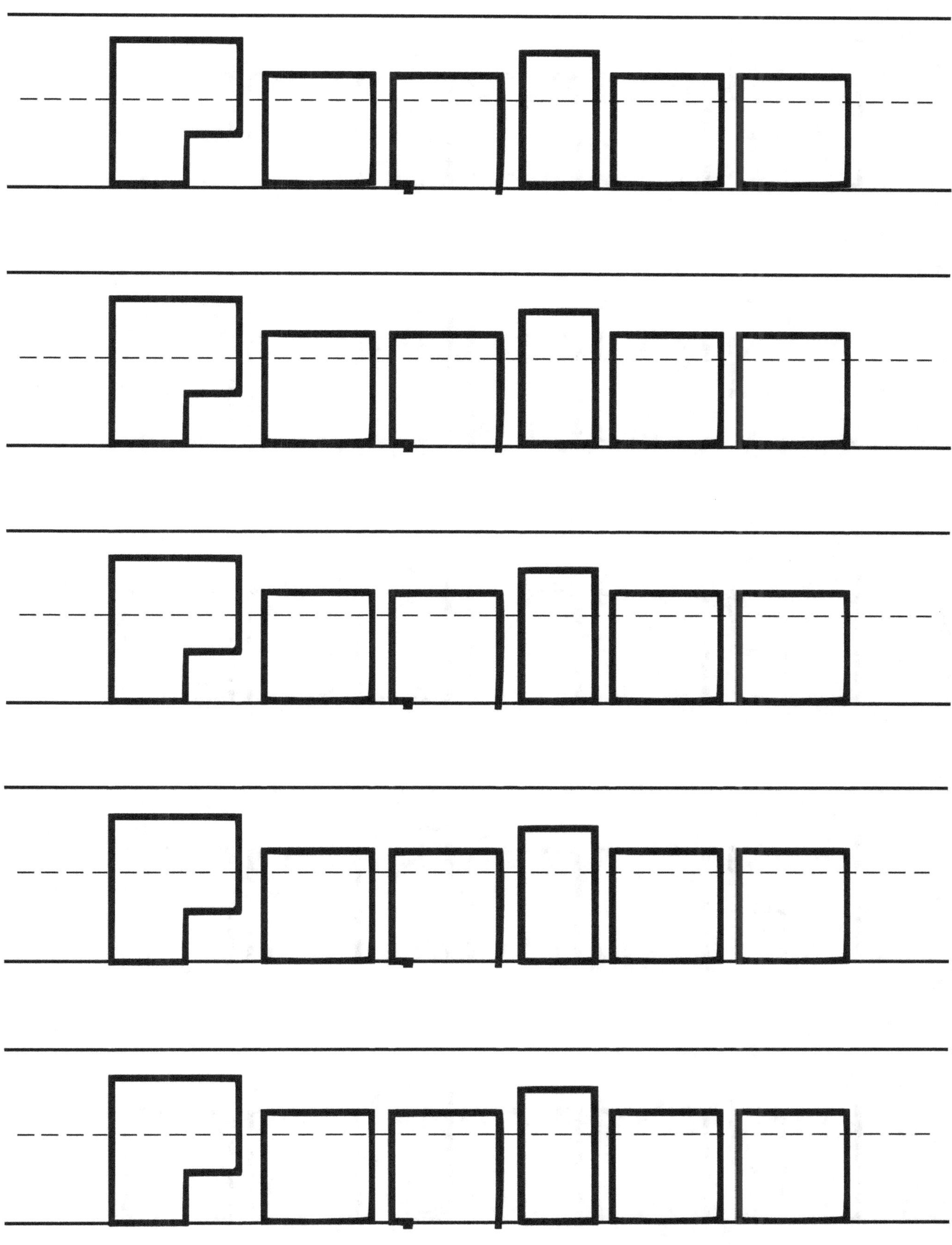

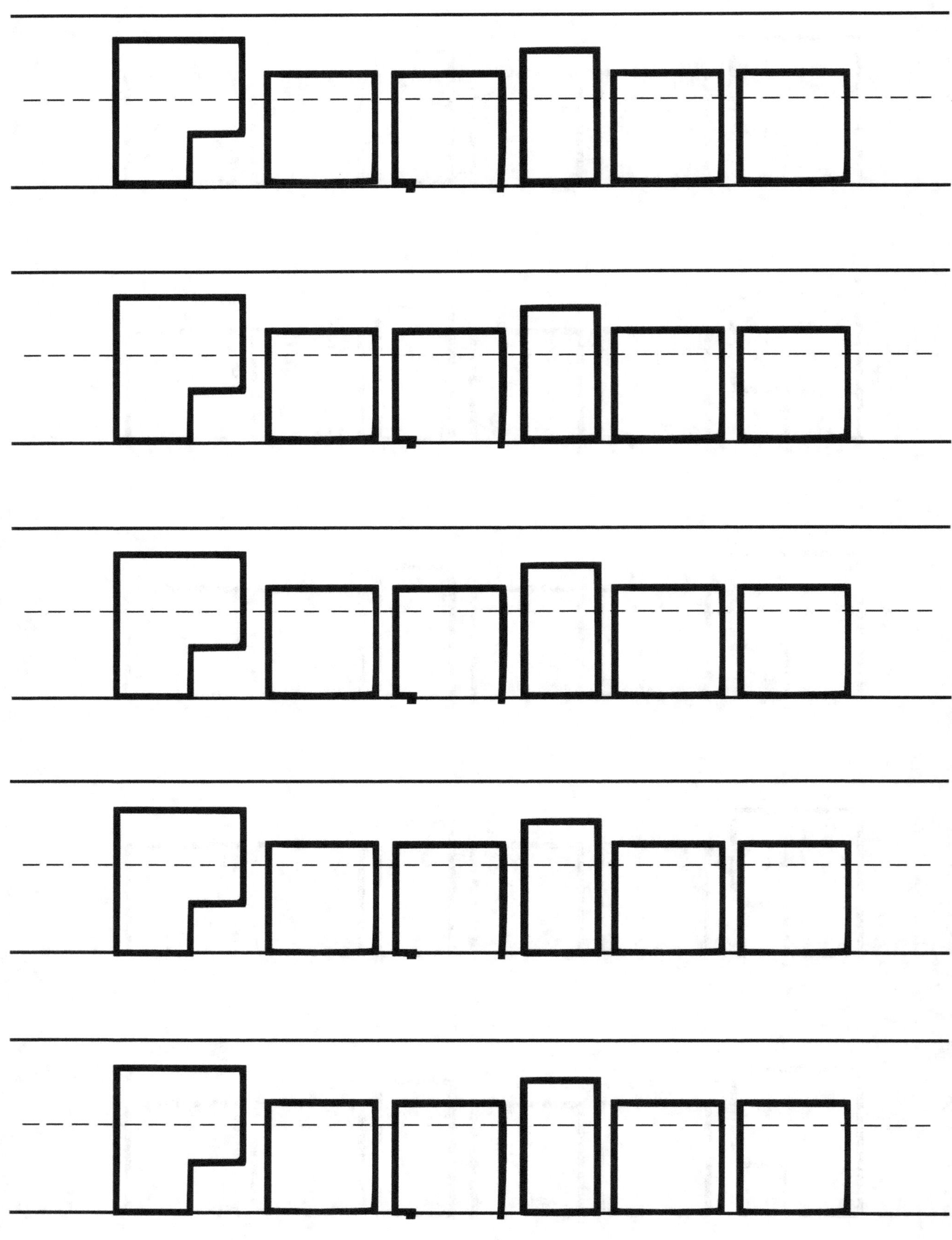

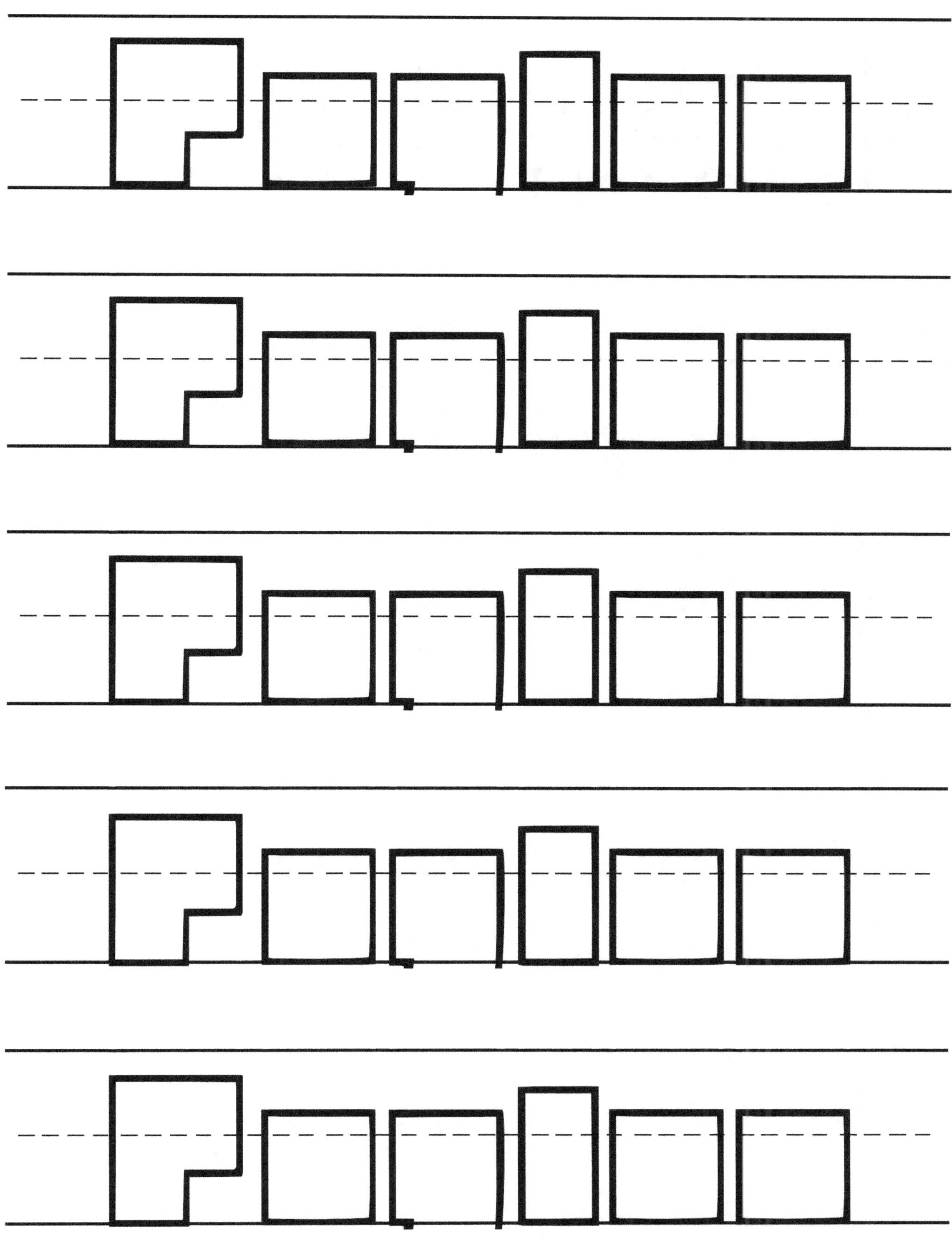

Peyton

Peyton

Peyton

Peyton

Peyton

Peyton

Peyton

Peyton

Peyton

Peyton

Peyton

Peyton

Peyton

Peyton

Peyton

Peyton

Peyton

Peyton

Peyton

Peyton

Peyton

Peyton

Peyton

Peyton

Peyton

Peyton

Peyton

Peyton

Peyton

Peyton

Peyton

Peyton

Peyton

Peyton

Peyton

Peyton

Peyton

Peyton

Peyton

Peyton

Peyton